MY THORN

A VIETNA.. ....

SPEAKS ABOUT

POST TRAUMATIC STRESS DISORDER

AND THE BIBLE

Published by

BOLIGA Publishers

38 Bishop Road NW

Cartersville, GA 30121-7386

770-382-7607

boliga@juno.com

bdgayton@juno.com

Copyright, 2011

Bobby D. Gayton

ISBN 978-1-257-9134-7

TABLE OF CONTENTS

DEDICATION

My Family

There have been many who have helped me in my struggle with Post Traumatic Stress Disorder (PTSD). First of all, this book is dedicated to my wife, Linda. Her father suffered from Post Traumatic Stress Disorder from World War 2. It should not have been her lot in life to have married a man who would suffer from Post Traumatic Stress Disorder. She is the light of my life. She knows and has seen the struggles, the night sweats, dreams, flashbacks, tears and all of the symptoms of Post Traumatic Stress Disorder manifested in my life. She has been there when I was struggling with closure. She was there when we found and visited with the families of my "brothers" that were killed in Vietnam. Second, to my children, Brooke, Jason, and Jonathan I can only seek your forgiveness and understanding for having to live with me as I struggled with Post Traumatic Stress Disorder as a Christian, father, and preacher. Third, to my mother, my "hero" who passed from this life at the age of 92 on April, 9th, 2011, my three sisters and my three brothers who have tried to understand me. Fourth, I give my heartfelt gratitude to members of the Cartersville church of Christ for their prayers and encouragement as they watched their preacher come to grips with Post Traumatic Stress Disorder. And finally, to Bobby Wood who has been that special friend with whom I could call and talk with as I struggle with Post Traumatic Stress Disorder. Many of his calls were at "the right time."

Brothers Forever

To those who have struggled and been there, my "brothers" of the Vietnam Veterans of Bartow County Georgia, "the group" and the men of Alpha Company (the Alphagators) 3rd Battalion 22nd Infantry of the 3rd Brigade of the 25th Infantry Division, the following words from an unknown author describe my feelings for you.

Men Who Have Been To War

"I now know why men who have been to war yearn to reunite. Not to tell stories or look at old pictures. Not to laugh or weep. Comrades gather because they long to be with the men who once acted at their best; men who suffered and sacrificed together, who were stripped of their humanity. I did not pick these men. They were delivered by fate and the military. But I know them in a way I know no other men. I have never given anyone such trust. They were willing to guard something more precious than my life. They would have carried my reputation, the memory of me. It was part of the bargain we all made, the reason we were so willing to die for one another. As long as I have memory, I will think of them all, every day. I am sure that when I leave this world, my last thoughts will be of my family and my comrades… Such good men." (Author Unknown).

SGT Lowen Jones

Every year on February 7th I remember the sacrifice that was given so that I might live. Sergeant Lowen Jones died on this day in 1968 in the Village of Apo Cho. One of the hardest things that I have ever done in my life was to visit his brothers and sisters and meet his daughter. I went to comfort but was comforted by them. Jesus said, "Greater love hath no man than this, that a man lay down his life for his friends (John 15:13)." We are "brothers forever." The Vietnam Memorial Wall in Washington, D. C. carries his name at 38E 3.

My Vietnam "Brothers" That Gave All

SSGT Gary Maurice Brixen – NOV 21, 1967
SP4 Willard Thurman Bateman – NOV 21, 1967
CPL James Leonard Travis JR – NOV 22, 1967
SP4 Richard D. Harrison – DEC 14, 1967
PFC Ellsworth Swann – DEC 14, 1967
SP 4 Thomas Ellsworth Layne JR – DEC 22, 1967
PFC Ennis Crowe – JAN 1, 1968
SP4 Abel Croom Stroud – JAN 1, 1968

SP4 James W. McCaffrey – JAN 2, 1968
SP4 Samuel Rivera-Fernandez – JAN 2, 1968
SGT Larry Wright – JAN 27, 1968
SGT Rube A. Cox JR - JAN 27, 1968
PFC Lester S. Kinard – JAN 29, 1968
SP4 Robert W. Neher – JAN 29, 1968
SP4 Edward McCorvey JR– FEB 3, 1968
SGT Lowen Leon Jones – FEB 7, 1968
PFC Gary Christenbury – FEB 10, 1968
SP4 Dennis Hahn – FEB 18, 1968
SGT Francisco Franco – MAR 3, 1968
SP4 Vincent A. Datena - MAR 3, 1968
SP4 William A. Jordon – MAR 3, 1968
SP4 Jimmie Leheman – MAR 3, 1968
SP4 Jimmie Edward Parker – MAR 3, 1968
SP4 Michael H. Pennell – MAR 3, 1968
SP4 Richard C. Spencer – MAR 3, 1968
SP4 Robert L. Melton – APR 12, 1968
PFC Michael Cacciuttolo – APR 23, 1968
CPL Harry L. Sowell – APR 23, 1968
SP4 Conley Arlen Bradshaw – JUNE 2, 1968
SP4 James Ray Moncrief - AUG 18, 1968
SP4 Gilbert T. Delgado – AUG 18, 1968
SGT James Kraynak – AUG 18, 1968
PFC Paul O'Leary – AUG 22, 1968

Chapter 1

My Story

My name is Bobby D. Gayton and I suffer from Post Traumatic Stress Disorder because of my service in the Vietnam War. Before giving the facts of my one year tour in Vietnam the following are the events that led up to my entering the U.S. Army. The war in Vietnam was going on while I was a senior at Cass High School in Cartersville Georgia. Some of those with whom I had classes had already entered the military and were headed for Vietnam. On September 24th 1965 I met my future wife Linda S. Smith, a senior from Cartersville High School, at the Bartow County Fair sponsored by the American Legion Post 42. After graduation Linda and I began to date. We became engaged in October of 1966. We spent a lot of time talking about our future including Vietnam. I received that "Uncle Sam" letter and went for my physical. I passed the physical and was given a 1A status to be drafted. We finally decided that we would wait to be married until my tour in Vietnam was over. In February I went to the draft board and told them that I wanted to be drafted the next month so that I could start my two year hitch. They accommodated me and sent me down in March, but they forgot to send my paperwork so I was sent back for another month. On April 3rd, 1967 I was sworn into the U. S. Army as a Private E1. I was given three choices as to where I wanted to be stationed. I chose Alaska, Hawaii, and Vietnam. Why Vietnam? I knew that I would end up going there. Basic Training was at Fort Benning Georgia for eight weeks where I trained with Echo Company 10th Battalion, 3rd Brigade. At the end of basic training I was promoted to Private E2.

During this time my family and Linda visited when they could. During my seventh week I began to work in the Orderly Room. My Company Commander asked if I would like to spend my two years as company clerk. I gladly said "YES!" But before they could get the orders changed I was on my way to Fort Polk Louisiana for eight more weeks of Advanced Infantry Training. I was now going to be introduced to infamous Tiger Land. The majority of our training here was to prepare us for Vietnam. At the end of my training I was promoted to Private First Class (E3).

My first cousin Tommy Hufsteller was killed in Vietnam on June 30th, 1967. I was not able to attend his funeral to say good-bye; little did I know that death would become a "way of life" in Vietnam.

With my training finished I went home for a thirty day leave. I spent most of my time with Linda and my family. I left the Atlanta airport on September 1st for Fort Ord, California to be processed to Vietnam. I left Fort Ord on September 4th on my "senior trip", stopping on Wake Island for fuel before arriving at Cam Ranh Bay, Vietnam.

After spending the night I flew to Camp Alpha in Saigon. A few days later I was sent by convoy to Chu Chi where I stayed for about a week attending "in country" training. I then was flown to Dau Tieng to join my unit, Alpha Company of the 3rd Battalion, 3rd Brigade, and 22nd Infantry of the 25th Infantry Division. Dau Tieng was a base camp that was in the Tay Ninh Province and part of the Michelin Rubber Plantation was located there. Dau Tieng received mortars from the Viet Cong every day. I worked for two or three days at the 3rd Brigade headquarters as a typist. I was asked if I wanted to spend my tour in Vietnam at headquarters. My answer was a quick, "YES." But this assignment did not come to pass.

My First Sergeant sent me to the field where Alpha Company was dug in for the night. The first person I met in the field was Specialist Four, Lowen Jones, a red-headed freckle faced man just like me. He said, "I'm Jones from East Saint Illinois and I will be your squad leader." And I said, "I'm Gayton from Cartersville Georgia." Jones had been in Vietnam since late March. His first concerns were about my going home in September of 1968, i.e., staying alive until then. He informed me that if I wanted to return to Georgia that I must pay attention and learn from those who had "been there and done that." Jones had learned a lot from those who had survived the battle of "Soui Tre" which had taken place in March 1967. He stated that "if we get hit today do what you can but don't try to be a hero." We got hit and the Drill Sergeants were right when they told us that in the first "fire fight" your whole life will pass before you. Bullets were bouncing all around where I had fallen. From that day forward I watched and listened to all of my peers. Jones was a good teacher and was always willing to answer questions and give advice. He truly was a leader in every sense of the word.

Before I left Cartersville Georgia, Linda gave me a diary so that I could write in it every day, but I did not begin until about two months later after arriving in Vietnam. The following events are taken from this diary combined with the letters that I wrote home. Some of the events were updated from other materials that I got from the archives. These events are described so that the reader may understand about "my thorn in the flesh" – Post Traumatic Stress Disorder.

*November 21, 196*7. We are on Operation Diamond Head. We came upon a Viet Cong base camp. As we were fighting my former platoon sergeant, Staff Sergeant Gary Maurice Brixen from Ossed, WI was killed. He had just returned from seeing his wife in Hawaii. Upon his return he was assigned to another platoon. Specialist Four Williard Thurman Bateman from Bullard, TX, our medic, was also killed. Specialist Four Dirkin and Specialist Four Chestrick were wounded. Air strikes were called in on the Viet Cong. The thoughts that were going through my mind were that we all were going to be killed. There were Viet Cong bunkers and mines everywhere. The Viet Cong had tunnels dug to the bunkers so that they could retreat to another bunker or escape.

November 22, 1967. We are still in the same area. We went on an ambush patrol and we placed toilet paper on the mines so that no one would step on them. There was no sleep that night. Corporal James Leonard Travis JR from Shelbyville, KY is killed. Private First Class Guerou and our company commander Captain Williams were wounded. Captain Curt Chancey was sent out to be our new company commander. This was Captain Chancey's second tour of duty in Vietnam. I and the others who served with him owe him our lives. I kept thinking that if these kinds of battles are going to happen every day, all of us would be killed or wounded before this operation was over. Our supplies and ammo were running low. Those traumatic two days made a mark in my mind. I will not forget the sounds of mines, grenades, bombs exploding, the screams and the facial expressions of those around me.

December 2, 1967. I am promoted to Specialist Four (E4).

December 13, 1967. We are now on Operation Yellowstone. We were told that we would be out for fifty eight days, but this was not so. We only stayed out five days.

December 14, 1967. Specialist Four Richard D. Harrison and PFC Ellsworth Swann are killed.

December 17, 1967. Today we came upon an old Viet Cong base camp. The Viet Cong had built another base camp on our right flank with tunnels to the old base camp. Our point squad was allowed by the Viet Cong to go through before they ambushed us. Our Forward Observer and a "new man" were killed and 9 others were wounded. In my mind I kept asking myself, "Is this going to happen every time we go out?" I helped load our wounded and the two KIA's on the chopper. It seems that death is all around us. I kept thinking that I would never see the wounded again unless they were sent back to our company. Did any of the wounded die? I do not know. I kept thinking about all that had happened since November 21. My fears of being killed, wounded, maimed, and even being captured began to keep me awake. I sought "pills" from the medic so that I could mix them with our "nightly" can of beer so that I could sleep. I become the platoon sergeant's Radio Operator. The reason for this was that I am color blind. It was hard for me to see the difference in the tints of the bushes, etc. So, the squad leader did not want me to walk point for him anymore.

December 19, 1967. We have been in the Hobo Woods for four days. Our new platoon sergeant, Staff Sergeant Hufacker, Private First Class Kimbrell, Sergeant Jones, Private First Class Drew, Specialist Four "Doc" Jennies, and Specialist Four Byrum are wounded. We came upon a Viet Cong base camp. Kimbrell and I fell on top of a bunker. The Viet Cong on the inside were throwing out grenades. They even threw ours back at us. In basic training we were taught how to use the grenade. I took my grenade, pulled the pin and held it for three seconds and then threw it in the bunker killing those inside. During all of this Kimbrell, Drew, and "Doc" Jennies were wounded from the grenades that were being thrown back at us. One of our platoon members "cracked up" during the fire-fight but later I found out that he had a seizure. All of the noises could not drown out the screaming from the wounded. The Viet Cong had waited until we were right on top of them before they sprang their ambush

December 23, 1967. This was a terrible day for me. Specialist Four Thomas Elsworth Layne JR from Chattanooga, TN was killed. We had met at Advanced Infantry Training in Fort Polk, LA. He was divorced but had a little girl that he talked about daily. As we were moving through an open area a "short artillery round" fell into our ranks. Layne was killed and 3 others were wounded. We have lost so many people that now we are about half strength. My thoughts were "Will I be next." Not only are we dealing with the Viet Cong, and the North Vietnamese Army, but now I am afraid of our own artillery.

December 24, 1967. There is a "cease fire" because it is Christmas. We are sent on a day-time ambush patrol. On this day I walked point. As we were walking through the jungle we heard a rushing noise coming toward us. I knew that we were all going to be killed. I thought that we had come upon a Viet Cong base camp. But we had actually come upon four wild boars! Funny now! But not then! I was thankful that no one fired a round. I did not volunteer for point again.

December 31, 1967. We are now on the second phase of Operation Yellowstone. We have been sent to set up Fire Support Base Burt. During the night we are probed by the North Vietnamese Army. One of our machine gun positions kills two of their soldiers. When morning came I called in my Listening Post. As they were coming in a North Vietnamese Army soldier stood up between us. Sergeant Franco yells "shoot him." But I could not because I was afraid that I might hit one of the Listening Post members. I also feared as we took him prisoner that he might have a mine or grenade strapped to his body. He did have a pistol. During the day the Prisoner Of War was interrogated and he informed those who were interrogating him that there were others and that we were going to be attacked. Captain Chancey told us to dig in deeper. Specialist Kanter and I did as we were told. We dug our foxhole deeper and surrounded our foxhole with sand bags. Specialist Four Abel Croom Stroud III is killed.

January 1, 1968. The battle of Sui Cut began about 7 PM. We came under massive enemy ground and mortar attack. It was estimated that we were hit by four regiments of the North Vietnamese Army and Viet Cong soldiers. Charlie Company's ambush patrol sustained fifty percent wounded and one killed. During the night Alpha and Charlie companies were hit hard. Our perimeters were under threat of being overrun. We had North Vietnamese Army soldiers inside our perimeter before the night was over. The bunker to my left was evacuated by its members because they ran out of ammo. Three bunkers to my right Charlie Company was being overrun. The artillery behind us began firing 105MM and 155MM at point blank range to stop the North Vietnamese Army from overrunning our positions. During all of this I had been hit with shrapnel on my leg. My Listening Post was in trouble all night. But finally around 5 AM we got them back inside the perimeter. Specialist Four Alford was wounded and would lose a leg. Sergeant Miller could not hear and Sergeant Jones was temporarily blinded. Specialist Four Alford was "going home." We were consistently hit with the North Vietnamese Army mortar fire, Rocket Propelled Grenade rounds, and small arms. The artillery had to fire "beehive" rounds (a bomb with darts inside) to route the enemy from our bunker line. We had gunships, "puff the magic dragon," B52 bombers, etc., dropping everything they had and as close to us as they could in order to stop the enemy. Alpha lost two more men and I don't know how many of us were wounded. Helicopters kept coming in dropping supplies.

When morning came, Alpha and Charlie companies were air lifted to Katum, but we returned the next day to patrol around Fire

Support Base Burt. I saw swollen bodies. The smell was unreal. The artillery dug a grave and we placed hundreds of bodies in it. This burial haunted me until 2007 when I finally had to deal with it in a counseling session. We were told by those in the sky that there were blood trails leading away from Fire Support Base Burt in every direction. This event made a change in me. The scars are still there even until this day. I began to drink a lot and sought more "pills" from the medics. Anything that I thought would take the memories away and help me sleep. But nothing helped. Later I learned that the mechanized unit that was with us, the 2nd of the 22nd (Triple Deuce), was going to leave us that day, but for some reason they did not. If they had, many of us would not be alive today. We were put in for a Presidential Unit Citation, and we received an Army Commendation Medal with a "V" device for valor and the Vietnam Cross of Gallantry with Palm Unit Citation Badge.

Later a movie would be made about the events of this day. The title of the movie is "Platoon." But the movie was made in Hollywood and later Captain Dye wrote the novelization of Oliver Stone's script, *Close Quarters*. Oliver Stone did serve with Bravo Company during the time of this battle. There are two books that have been written by those who were there. Captain Robert Hemphill wrote the book, *Platoon – Bravo Company* and Charles J. Boyle wrote the book *Absolution – Charlie Company 3rd Battalion, 22nd Infantry*. Lieutenant Boyle served with Alpha Company from August 1967 to January 1968 as the Platoon Leader of third platoon. He became the Company Commander of Charlie Company after this battle. Specialist Four James W. McCaffrey, Private First Class Ennie E. Crow and Specialist Four Samuel Rivera-Fernandez are killed.

January 3, 1968. We are at Katum. We are now conducting reconnaissance in the area surrounding Katum. I take my first "hot" shower since being in Vietnam. "Doc" takes care of my leg wound.

January 4, 1968. We receive incoming fire at Katum.

January 5, 1968. We are airlifted back to Dau Tieng. I got all of my mail from home and spent the afternoon reading and writing letter back home. Some of the men were smoking pot and encouraged me to try it. I did and cried myself to sleep because I missed Linda and my family.

January 6, 1968. We are in the Michelin Rubber Plantation. We stopped a truck that had seven Vietnamese aboard. We found a map of the Michelin Rubber Plantation.

January 7, 1968. We are airlifted to Fire Support Base Burt. We receive mortar rounds from the enemy. We had two wounded.

January 9, 1968. We are still at Fire Support Base Burt. We are heavily mortared. One of the Lieutenants and his Radio Operator are wounded. I kept thinking that before this operation is over we all will be killed or wounded. The loud noises of the mortars are terrifying and the "tube sound" never leaves.

January 12, 1968. We are still at Fire Support Base Burt. We leave on a sweep mission. We came upon on an old enemy base camp. We found about one hundred and fifty foxholes that the enemy had dug. We remain at Fire Support Base Burt until January 22nd.

January 23, 1968. We are airlifted back to Dau Tieng to conduct operations in the Michelin Rubber Plantation. One person is wounded from a booby trap. We return to the base camp. Reflections over the past three months bring loneliness. Many of my friends from Fort Polk have been wounded or killed. I have gotten to the point that I do not want to see any of those that I knew before Vietnam because they tell me about someone who was with us at Fort Polk being killed or wounded. I kept thinking, "Who will be next." I tried smoking pot for the second time. This time I wanted to steal a "huey" (helicopter) and go home. I never smoked pot anymore.

January 27, 1968. We left Dau Tieng on the 26th and will not return until March 30th, 1968. The TET (Vietnam's New Year) Offensive began. When we returned to Dau Tieng all of my personal items had been stolen by other soldiers. Today Sergeant

Larry Wright from Jacksonville, FL was killed. He was always singing with the other members of the machine gun crew, McCorvey and Johnson, while we were digging our foxholes. Sergeant Rube A. Cox JR was killed. Who will be next?

January 29, 1968. Private First Class Lester S. Kinard and Specialist Four Robert W. Neher were killed.

February 3, 1968. We got to the village of Ap Cho on the 2nd, but tonight we went on a night march. We had to get to Cu Chi because there was the possibility that the Viet Cong and the North Vietnamese Army were going to take over the city of Cu Chi. This was a very scary trip. We had never done this before. As we went down Highway 1 we had to go through an ARVN (the South Vietnamese Army) outpost. When we got on the other side I heard a shot. I fell to the side of the road like all the others. My left knee was bleeding and numb from the fall. We began to ask if everyone was okay. Specialist Four Edward McCorvey JR from Pensacola, FL was killed. We never fired a round! I have always believed that the ARVN (the South Vietnamese Army) outpost shot at us and killed McCorvey. From that day forward I did not trust the ARVN's (the South Vietnamese Army). We went to base camp at Cu Chi.

February 4, 1968. We walked through the fields to the city of Cu Chi under fire from the enemy. On the other side of the Cu Chi the ARVN (the South Vietnamese Army) outpost was destroyed. We fought openly in the fields on the other side of Cu Chi. The Major who was an advisor for the ARVN's (the South Vietnamese Army) and his Radio Operator had been killed. We were picked up at dusk and carried to the Cu Chi base camp where we received heavy mortar fire all night. We placed the Major's and his Radio Operator's bodies on our chopper. At the Cu Chi base camp we got into a big underground bunker and played cards (gambled) nearly all night. I won a lot of money but had no place to spend it!

February 5, 1968. We go back to AP Cho. We continue to fight the Viet Cong and the North Vietnamese Army in the village. They are on one side of the road and we are on the other. They had well built bunkers behind the village. We are instructed not to destroy the village.

February 7, 1968. Today was the hardest day that I had in Vietnam. After the events of that day I knew I would never be the same. We had returned to the village of Ap Cho and continued to fight the well entrenched Viet Cong and North Vietnamese Army. This village was also called "The Village of Tears." We had been fighting with the enemy since returning to the village. First platoon was told to take a squad up into the area where we thought the bunkers were. We were to get as close as we could so that we could call in artillery. Being the platoon sergeant's Radio Operator I was assigned to Sergeant Jones' squad. Sergeant Jones took point and I followed. We had gotten closer to the bunkers than anyone else in the past few days. But Sergeant Jones wanted to get closer so that we could make sure the artillery was destroying the bunkers. Once in position, Sergeant Jones motioned for me to come to him. As I left my position and started toward him he stood and motioned for me to get down. A Rocket Propelled Grenade round went past my head as I was jumping behind cover, exploding behind me. I was hit with shrapnel on the right side of my face. Sergeant Jones was shot. We were told to move back but we said, "No." We had never left anyone. Specialist Four Wilkie's machine gun crew and the medic got to Sergeant Jones. The medic worked with him while we laid down continuous fire. Sergeant Jones died after being brought back to life twice. We returned to our perimeter. The medic wanted to send me in because of the wound to my face and because of my emotional state. I refused to go. Captain Chancey speaks to me with tears in his eyes as he observes Sergeant Jones' body. I was able to stay in the field, but did not go out with the others for a day or so.

In April of 1968 I finally wrote home and told my family and Linda what had happened. I am alive today because of what he did and taught me. Sergeant Jones received the Silver Star and another Purple Heart that day. For days I felt numb. In the next two days two more were killed and five wounded. One of them died waiting for the "dust off" (medical evacuation by helicopter). "When will this end?" were my thoughts. We only have twenty men left in first platoon. It is hard to understand why we cannot blow up this village and destroy the bunkers. A convoy comes through in about two days. The Viet Cong and the North Vietnamese Army opened fire and the mechanized unit did a right face and leveled the village. If this had happened days before just maybe Sergeant Jones and the others would be alive today. It was not until January 2nd, 2001 that I was awarded the Purple Heart for the wound on the right side of my face.

February 10, 1968. Private First Class Gary Christenbury was killed.

February 18, 1968. SP4 Dennis Hahn from the fourth platoon was killed.

March 1, 1968. Alpha Company is removed from Apo Cho. We are put in for another Presidential Unit Citation for the battle of Apo Cho. Forty-four Americans died at Apo Cho, the "Village of Tears." We are sent to the Saigon River to patrol. My thoughts were "finally some rest." This was a disastrous move.

March 3, 1968. Sergeant Francisco Franco, Specialist Four William A. Jordon, Specialist Four Vincent A. Datena, Specialist Four Jimmie Lehman, Specialist Four Jimmie E. Parker, Specialist Four Michael H. Pennell, and Specialist Four Richard C. Spencer drown. Our instructions were to keep all of our gear on at all times. Sergeant Franco was unable to get on the boat with the rest of his squad so he got on the last boat. The boat turned over and there was nothing that we could do. Sergeant Franco had about thirty four days left before going home. I always thought that Sergeant Franco's body was never found but I was told in May of 1997 by Captain Chancey that his body was found two weeks later.

Nothing I try to do erases the memories. I just cannot get Jones, Wright, and Travis, Layne and now Franco and all the others off my mind. I began to lose a lot of sleep. I just cannot close my eyes without seeing my "brothers" who have died. My mixture of beer and now Darvon did not help. I become a squad leader, giving up my Radio Operator duties. We were short of men. My squad begins to ride up and down the Saigon River on a large gunboat at night looking for the Viet Cong who were moving supplies up and down the river. This type of ambush was something new and our unit was one of the first units to use this tactic.

March 10, 1968. I have lost a lot of sleep for the past three days. Because of my loss of sleep I had fallen asleep on an ambush patrol and now was in trouble with the LT (Lieutenant). I was relieved of my squad and was a Radio Operator again. Later, after receiving my "rights" read to me I was told to give the radio to Specialist Four Byrum because I was going in to Dau Tieng to receive an Article 15 or court martial. Our Lieutenant was leaving to become the Executive Officer back at Dau Tieng so now we had a new Lieutenant. First platoon was sent on patrol. They came upon some bunkers and a fire fight began. Staff Sergeant Coleman, Specialist Four Byrum, and Specialist Four Hall were wounded. The wounded were dusted off (medical evacuation by helicopter). First platoon returned to the perimeter and reported to Captain Chancey. Captain Chancey told the Lieutenant to find me and put me on the radio.

When I called Captain Chancey I was told to re-group what was left of first platoon and return to the area where the fire fight had taken place. Specialist Four Rash volunteered to be my Radio Operator. Specialist Four James Moncrief volunteered to be my point man. As we arrived I radioed Captain Chancey and he called in artillery. We walked the artillery in so close that it threw debris all over us. I could smell the powder and smoke. I also remembered the "short round" that killed Thomas Layne. I called for Specialist Tripp to come up so that he could use the LAW's (light antitank weapon) and blow up the bunkers. Tripp was the best we had at firing this weapon. After the bunkers were blown up we began to search them. We found one KIA but then Captain Chancey ordered us out of the area. The area was heavily booby trapped. Specialist Rash was wounded while we were blowing up the bunkers. Captain Chancey re-assured me that I would not be receiving an Article 15 or a court martial.

April 1, 1968. Thirty-three of us from Alpha Company receive the Combat Infantryman Badge (First Award).

April 8, 1968. Operation Toan Thang begins and will last until May 31st, 1968. This was an operation that took us through the woods and jungles, wading through rice paddies, and slogging through swamps.

April 9, 1968. First Platoon was sent to the Hoc Mon Bridge for security. We received sniper fire. The next morning the South Vietnamese sent out a patrol to check out the area. One of the soldiers brought back the head of the Viet Cong that was killed.

April 12, 1968. Specialist Four Robert Melton was killed.

April 23, 1968. Corporal Harry Sowell and Private First Class Michael Cacciuttolo were killed. Two others were wounded. At this time I quit writing in the diary. I came to the conclusion that if I did not write down what was happening it would all go away, but it did not. I also stopped writing home and only answered letters that I received. It is during this time that Alpha, Bravo, and Delta Companies are sent to join Charlie Company in the Catholic Village. While here we had time to heal and get back to company strength. As we continue to patrol, First Platoon got to go into the village and help our medics with giving aid to those who were sick and injured. What I saw was heartbreaking. Our medic treated a small child who had the mumps. Someone had lanced them thinking that they were something else.

June 8, 1968. I am in Dau Tieng after being on a much needed seven day R&R (Rest and Relaxation) to Taiwan. While in Taiwan I got to call and talk to Linda and my mother. When I returned to Dau Tieng the first thing I learned was that Specialist Four Conely Arlen Bradshaw from Church Hill, TN was killed on June 2nd. I was told that our platoon had gotten hit and as he was firing at the Viet Cong the machine gun jammed. I felt like a part of me had died. We had been through so much together. His wife's name was Linda. I did not get to say good-bye. I'm scared! My thoughts were that I had to get out of the field. I had come to realize that when my "brothers" died that a part of me was dying with them. I'm drinking a lot and taking "pills" to forget. The "shorter" I have gotten the more frightened I have become. It seems that we have lost a lot of men with 60 days or less left. I only have 88 days left. Will I make it?

I am sent to Leadership Training School in Chu Chi. they needed someone to go from our company and I was the "lucky" man in the company area at that time. It was good for me to go there.

July 4, 1968. We are away from Dau Tieng. The base camp was attacked with over four hundred rocket and mortar rounds. Two Viet Cong companies launched a suicidal attack. The Viet Cong were inside the perimeter before the attack was halted. One of the Viet Cong that was killed and found in the wire was the barber on the base camp. He had cut my hair and shaved my face!

July 5, 1968. I was promoted to Sergeant (E5). During the days ahead I was brought in from the field. I began to drive jeeps to Tay Ninh and Chu Chi. On one of these trips the jeep I was driving stopped running. I was left on the side of the road until the last jeep came and hooked up to my jeep. I kept thinking about being an easy target for the enemy.

August 17, 1968. I have only thirteen days left. With five other "short timers" we volunteered to go outside Tay Ninh to Fire Support Base Buell II and have bunker guard so that others could get some rest. About 10 PM we were hit by the Viet Cong and the North Vietnamese Army. The Battle of Tay Ninh had begun. They tried to overrun our position but failed. The artillery, knowing we were "short timers" and had volunteered for bunker guard so that they could rest, told us if we are hit for us to get in the foxhole and keep our heads down. They fired point blank into the on charging Viet Cong and the North Vietnamese Army. When morning came there were bodies in front of our bunker. I was so scared that I shook with the other "short timers." During the night as I looked up at Nui Ba Den – the Black Virgin Mountain – I saw that Alpha Company was also getting hit. Fog was on the mountain so they could not get any support.

When I returned to Tay Ninh the next day I saw the Lieutenant and he told me that five were killed and twenty-three were wounded. The objective of the enemy was to destroy the Signal Facility. I tried to find those that were left from my squad. I found Doug and he told me that Specialist Four James Moncrief from Cordova, AL was killed. Moncrief back on March 10th had become my point man and a vital part of my squad. He had been appointed squad leader just that day. I only had twelve days left but I thought that I would lose it. All I wanted to do was leave Vietnam and FORGET! But I would never forget. Also Specialist Four Gilbert T. Delgado and Sergeant James C. Kraynak were killed. Many of those that I had served with were severely wounded and sent out of Vietnam. Others were taken out of the field and given other things to do because of what they went through on top of the mountain. Back in September of 1967 when I got to Alpha Company I was given a "special" calendar to mark off the days. The last twelve days were never marked off. I do not recall nine of the days. Two of the last three days were spent at Camp Alpha and my last day at Long Binh. At Camp Alpha Sergeant Holly and I were treated to a steak dinner and all that we could drink by the Air Force NCO club. We were the "shortest" of the "short-timers" present on that night.

There are other events that took place but I do not remember the dates. I do not know why I quit writing in my diary; unless I felt like I had told those back home enough. Before Sergeant Jones was killed, one of our squad leaders was Sergeant Miller. He was moving our squad across an open area when we came upon a Viet Cong bunker. The Viet Cong pinned us down and the only thing that we could do was to charge the bunker. Sergeant Miller tried to fire a LAW (a light antitank weapon) and it exploded blinding him. I never saw him after that. The Viet Cong was killed. Sometime before February 7th, 1968, Sergeant Jones tells us that we have made twenty-five air assaults. We were later told that we would not receive any "wings" because we were not an air assault unit.

Sometime during the monsoon (rainy) season I and two others were sent out on LP (Listening Post). We went out and found a place that we thought was "fitting for the occasion." When we went on LP (Listening Post) we took turns listening and sleeping. While I was sleeping it started to rain – I mean RAIN! When I woke up, I was two feet from where I went to sleep. Funny now, but WET then!

It should be noted that some of the dates that I have given are the dates that I wrote in my diary. It should also be noted that I mentioned a lot of my "brothers" that were killed that were in the other platoons. I did not know them as well as I did those in first platoon, but they were my "brothers" as well. Also I have tried to update the events with reports that I received from the archives.

Also, I have stated that our unit was put in for two Presidential Unit Citations. The criteria for the Presidential Unit Citation are:

> "The Presidential Unit Citation is awarded to units of the Armed Forces of the United States and co-belligerent nations for extraordinary heroism in action against an armed enemy occurring on or after 7 December 1941. The unit must display such gallantry, determination, and esprit de corps in accomplishing its mission under extremely difficult and hazardous conditions as to set it apart and above other units participating in the same campaign. The degree of heroism required is the same as that which would warrant award of a Distinguished Service Cross to an individual. Extended periods of combat duty or participation in a large number of operational missions, either ground or air is not sufficient. This award will normally be earned by units that have participated in single or successive actions covering relatively brief time spans. It is not reasonable to presume that entire units can sustain Distinguished Service Cross performance for extended time periods except under the most unusual circumstances. Only

on rare occasions will a unit larger than battalion qualify for award of this decoration."

I went to the archives and got the documents awarding both of these but somewhere between Vietnam and the United States Army, someone forgot to enter them into the records. Our unit was to receive these two awards for the battles at Fire Support Base Burt and Ap Cho.

We also received the Army Valorous Unit Award. The criteria for the Army Valorous Unit Award are:

"Units of the Armed Forces of the United States may be awarded The Army Valorous Unit Award for extraordinary heroism in action against an armed enemy on or after 3 August 1963. The action certifying the award must have been performed while involved in military operations involving conflict with an opposing foreign force or while serving with friendly foreign forces engaged in an armed conflict against an opposing armed force in which the United States is not a belligerent force. The degree of gallantry, determination, and esprit de corps necessary for the awarding of the Army Valorous Unit Award is of a lesser degree than that necessary to be awarded the Presidential Unit Citation. However, the recipient unit must have been recognized above and beyond other units participating in the same conflict for their actions under hazardous conditions in the achievement of its mission. The degree of heroism required is the same as that which would justify award of the Silver Star to an individual under similar circumstances. It is not enough to have been in combat duty for extended periods of time or to have participated in several operational ground or air missions. On most occasions the award is warranted when units have taken part in single or successive actions that cover comparatively short time spans. The actions required to be awarded the citation could not reasonably be performed for any extended time periods except under very unusual circumstances. Rarely will a unit larger than a battalion meet the qualifications for award of this decoration."

We have received this award.

During my tour in Vietnam Alpha Company was involved in four counteroffensive attacks. We received the Vietnam Service ribbon with four bronze service stars on it.

Years later I realized that I came home on a plane with a heart full of grief, conflict, and confusion. I also realized the joy of being alive even though I suffered from Post Traumatic Stress Disorder.

Upon Staff Sergeant Brixen's return from Hawaii to be with his wife on R&R (Rest & Relaxation) he told us, "you only have one life, make the best of it. You only have one life to live." I have tried to take his advice. But, feelings of guilt set in because I had left my "brothers". What would be their fate? Will we keep our promise of trying to stay in touch even after the war is over? Yes and no! Did I really want to know what happened to them? Yes, I did! Later I found most of those with whom I served or they found me.

My last battle was August 17th, 1968. I returned to San Francisco September 1st, 1968. I arrived in Atlanta, GA to meet my mother, brother, sister, and Linda September 2nd, 1968. I made the transition from Vietnam in 72 hours. Linda and I were married twenty-eight days after my last battle and fourteen days after leaving Vietnam. I had six months left to serve in the Army. I was stationed at Fort Benning Georgia with the S3 Training Unit. After being released I returned home to seek employment. In the next three years I would have three different employers. I left each of them twice during that time. I also started to college to study accounting. Linda and I become Christians on September 24th, 1970, five years to the date that we met. Our lives changed! I worked and studied accounting and the Bible. I wanted to go to college to study the

Bible. I chose to go to Memphis School of Preaching which was the work of the Knight Arnold Church of Christ and in July, 1973 we moved to Memphis, Tennessee. I was in school for six hours a day and had to study six hours at home. I preached at Hickory Flat, Mississippi and Hughes, Arkansas while attending Memphis School of Preaching. The congregation at Hughes grew and so did I. I worked and studied and never had time to think about my past. Going to Memphis School of Preaching saved my life and my soul. But my past would surface.

What is Post Traumatic Stress Disorder (PTSD)?

"The essential features of Posttraumatic Stress Disorder is the development of characteristic symptoms following exposure to an extreme traumatic stressor involving direct personal experience of an event that involves actual or threatened death or serious injury, or other threat to one's physical integrity; or witnessing an event that involves death, injury, or a threat to another person; or learning about unexpected or violent death, serious harm, or threat of death or injury experienced by a family member or other close associate.... The person's response to the event must involve intense fear, helplessness, or horror (or in children, the response must involve disorganized or agitated behavior).... The characteristic symptoms resulting from the exposure to the extreme trauma include persistent reexperiencing of the traumatic event...., persistent avoidance of stimuli associated with the trauma and numbing of general responsiveness...., and persistent symptoms of increased arousal.... The full symptom picture must be present for more than 1 month...and the disturbance must cause clinically significant distress or impairment in social, occupational, or other important areas of functioning." (*Diagnostic and Statistical Manual of*

Mental Disorder (DSM-IV), <u>Anxiety</u> <u>Disorders</u> 309.81
Posttraumatic Stress Disorder).

In 1998, the Veterans Administration was treating approximately five hundred thousand cases of Post Traumatic Stress Disorder. There are millions of other combat veterans suffering from Post Traumatic Stress Disorder. However, they have no idea what is causing their problems or what to do about it. How many can be added to this number from the wars in Iraq and Afghanistan? These do have a choice. Veterans can continue to deny that they have problems (multiple divorces, drinking, drugs, unemployable, no friends nor social activity, flashbacks, nightmares) or they can seek help.

One needs to remember that the tour of duty for the Vietnam veteran was one year but some served two or more tours. Veterans of Iraq and Afghanistan were/are being deployed three or four times. To get the picture, imagine experiencing one of the above "stressors" repeatedly for one year or more.

It is my prayer that this book will help all who are suffering from Post Traumatic Stress Disorder. It is my prayer that all may find the inner peace they so desire.

Chapter 2

The Apostle Paul And His Story

Who was Paul? He was "Circumcised the eighth day, of the stock of Israel, *of* the tribe of Benjamin, an Hebrew of the Hebrews; as touching the law, a Pharisee; Concerning zeal, persecuting the church; touching the righteousness which is in the law, blameless." (Philippians 3:5, 6). He was reared among those of the Dispersion at Tarsus in Cilicia. He was a Roman citizen. (Acts 16:37, 38). As Saul, he refuted the ideas that the Christ had risen and that the Law of Moses that he had so zealously upheld was set aside and of no future value. Saul's zeal drove him to persecute Christians. And he did with all the vigor and energy that he could get together. But, let us consider the changes that took place in his life.

Let us go back and look at the life of Saul, that is, Paul. Saul is first mentioned in Acts 7:58 where we are told, "And cast him [Stephen] out of the city, and stoned him: and the witnesses laid down their clothes at a young man's feet, whose name was Saul." Who was this man Saul? Why did they place their clothes at Saul's feet? In Acts 8:1-3 we learn,

> "And Saul was consenting unto his death. And at that time there was a great persecution against the church which was at Jerusalem; and they were all scattered abroad throughout the regions of Judaea and Samaria, except the apostles. And devout men carried Stephen to his burial, and made great lamentation over him. As for Saul, he made havock of the church, entering into every house, and haling men and women committed them to prison."

Saul's part in this persecution was to make "havock of the church" and to commit those who were followers of the Christ into prison. The word "havock" is from the Greek word, λυμαινω and means, "1 to affix a stigma to, to dishonour, spot, defile. 2 to treat shamefully or with injury, to ravage, devastate, ruin" (Strong G3075). This word is found in the Greek imperfect tense showing that Saul's persecution was a continual and repeated action of his and the middle voice showing that Saul "he himself" was actually involved in it. Paul, himself, was continually ravaging and bringing to ruin the church for which Jesus died. Paul stated,

> "Take heed therefore unto yourselves, and to all the flock, over the which the Holy Ghost hath made you overseers, to feed the church of God, which he hath purchased with his own blood" (Acts 20:28).

Luke wrote, "Praising God and having favour with all the people. And the Lord added to the church daily such as should be saved" (Acts 2:47). Since the church is made up the saved, Saul was persecuting the saved.

Then we see in Acts 9:1-3 Saul's continuous onslaught of the disciples of Christ.

> "And Saul, yet breathing out threatenings and slaughter against the disciples of the Lord, went unto the high priest, And desired of him letters to Damascus to the synagogues, that if he found any of this way, whether they were men or women, he might bring them bound unto Jerusalem."

The Greek word for "breathing out" is εμπνεω and means "1 to breathe in or on. 2 to inhale. 2A threatenings and slaughter were so to speak the element from which he drew his breath" (Strong G1709). It is noted that these "threatenings and slaughter," i.e. murder, were the continuous element from which Saul drew his breath. In Acts 9:4-5, Saul encounters our Lord.

> "And he fell to the earth, and heard a voice saying unto him, Saul, Saul, why persecutest thou me? And he said, Who art thou, Lord? And the Lord said, I am Jesus whom thou persecutest: it is hard for thee to kick against the pricks."

One thing we learn from this is that to persecute the church is to persecute Jesus. In addition, to persecute one of Jesus' disciples is to persecute Jesus. Saul was guilty of persecuting Christians and since Christians are the saved, he was guilty of persecuting the church for which Jesus died.

Saul was told what to do (Acts 9:4-18; 22:10-16; 26:14-20) and he obeyed the instructions of the Lord. When Saul said, "Who art thou Lord" and Jesus said, "I am Jesus [of Nazareth] whom thou persecutest…" Saul accepted the evidence. The apostle John stated,

> "And many other signs truly did Jesus in the presence of his disciples, which are not written in this book: But these are written, that ye might believe that Jesus is the Christ, the Son of God; and that believing ye might have life through his name" (John 20:30–31).

Saul believed that the One he saw on the Damascus road was Jesus the Christ, the Messiah. But then Saul was told to go into Damascus and he would be told "what thou must do." After three days of fasting and prayer Ananias came to Saul and told him, "And now why tarriest thou? arise, and be baptized, and wash away thy sins, calling on the name of the Lord" (Acts 22:16; Cf. John 16:13). Saul's sins, threats, slaughters [murders], persecutions of the church [disciples, Christians, the saved], and his sufferings were ALL washed away.

Now Saul could get on with his life and NEVER suffer from guilt, anger, and anxiety about his past. Now Saul would never have a DREAM about what he did to members of the Lord's church. Now Saul would never have a FLASHBACK to his prior life as a "blasphemer, and a persecutor, and injurious" (1 Timothy 1:13). It should be noted to the reader that the statement about no flashbacks is said in irony. Now Saul would never have to look upon himself as "CHIEF" of sinners. (1 Timothy 1:15).

The conclusion of his obedience meant that Saul would never have to LOOK BACK on his former life for he said,

> "Brethren, I count not myself to have apprehended: but *this* one thing *I do*, forgetting those things which are behind, and reaching forth unto those things which are before, I press toward the mark for the prize of the high calling of God in Christ Jesus" (Philippians 3:13, 14).

I thought that when I obeyed the gospel of the Christ that my past life was gone. GONE! Paul, lead by the Holy Spirit, wrote these words around AD 62 but he wrote 1 Timothy around AD 64/65. Paul said, "forgetting", the Greek word, $επιλανθανομαι$, which is in the middle voice and means, "1 to forget. 2 neglecting, no longer caring for. 2 forgotten, given over to oblivion, i.e., uncared for" (Strong G1950). But when Paul writes in 1 Timothy that he was a "blasphemer, and a persecutor, and injurious" and describes himself as "chief" of sinners, had Paul forgotten those things which are behind? Were they gone? I know Paul no longer cared for those memories of his past. Neither do I!

In Acts 22:3-5 Paul says,

> "I am verily a man *which am* a Jew, born in Tarsus, *a city* in Cilicia, yet brought up in this city at the feet of Gamaliel, *and* taught according to the perfect manner of the law of the fathers, and was zealous toward God as ye all are this day. And I persecuted this way unto the death, binding and delivering into prisons both men and women. As also the high priest doth bear me witness, and all the estate of the elders: from whom also I received letters unto the brethren, and went to Damascus, to bring them which were there bound unto Jerusalem, for to be punished."

In Galatians 1:14, Paul states, "And profited in the Jews' religion above many my equals in mine own nation, being more exceedingly zealous of the traditions of my fathers." How zealous was Paul?

> "I verily thought with myself, that I ought to do many things contrary to the name of Jesus of Nazareth. Which thing I also did in Jerusalem: and many of the saints did I shut up in prison, having received authority from the chief priests; and when they were put to death, I gave my voice against them. And I punished them oft in every synagogue, and compelled them to blaspheme; and being exceedingly mad against them, I persecuted them even unto strange cities" (Acts 26:9-11).

When I read I Timothy 1:13, 14 and Philippians 3:13, 14, Paul is saying that he will continually forget his past as the one who breathed out threats, slaughtered Christians, as a blasphemer, persecutor, injurious, and considering himself as the chief sinner and that he will continually press toward heaven. Since this is a continuous thing that Paul is going to be doing, he would never forget the past but he would continuously press toward heaven. Heaven is real and so is Paul's past. Now I understand what Paul meant. Paul is saying that he was not going to allow his past to keep him from claiming "the prize of the high calling of God in Christ Jesus" that is, heaven, for faithfully following the Lord. Paul replaces living in the past with living in the future. He is showing all of us who suffer from Post Traumatic Stress Disorder that the past will always be there but it should not keep us from attaining heaven as our final home.

But, knowing this does not take away Post Traumatic Stress Disorder and its symptoms – survivals guilt, depression, isolation, rage, avoidance of feelings, anger, anxiety, sleep disturbance and nightmares, and intrusive thoughts. Would what happened in Vietnam leave an indelible mark that I would not be able to erase? I found that I was tempting to dwell on the past because it had such a strong emotional pull. It takes a conscious effort to continually replace those thoughts and feelings with the desire and necessary effort to "press toward" heaven.

I recall that Linda was talking to someone and the subject of Post Traumatic Stress Disorder came up. That person's advice to me through her was "to carry it to the Lord and leave it there." My response to Linda was, "The next time you are talking with her ask her to remember the worst day of her life and multiply it by two hundred and seventy nine." Why did I use two hundred and seventy nine? That was the amount of time I spent away from the "safety" of a base camp. Those days were spent in the jungles, the rice paddies, the villages, the woods, the Saigon River, and the rubber plantations of South Vietnam looking for and fighting the Viet Cong and the North Vietnamese Army soldiers. Many people do not understand Post Traumatic Stress Disorder because they do not associate their bad emotional and physical experiences with Post Traumatic Stress Disorder. Many people do not understand what Vietnam did to the young men (average age 19) who were combat soldiers.

Some of the members of the church saw one of our young men, Jonathan Galloway, killed in front of our church building. He was hit by a car and died instantly. They saw the father, Scot, as he sat next to his young Christian son rubbing his hair. Their question was, "will this ever go away?" My response to them was "no." Later that year we gathered for our July 4th celebration to observe the fireworks across the street. When it was all over the Georgia State Patrol came with their flashing lights to direct traffic and many who had seen the accident became upset and had to leave. They and the father will forever suffer from Post Traumatic Stress Disorder.

Was Paul's extreme guilt one of his characteristics? Was it his guilt that provided the drive to cause a great degree of dedication to his Christian purpose? Does his reference to his guilt give evidence of some deep-seated feelings? The zeal that Paul had against Christians caused him to be a persecutor and the zeal he had for the cause of Christ caused him to be the persecuted. Paul had a strenuous time behind him and Paul bore marks of it in his body for life (Galatians 6:17). Paul's self-discipline was his chief strength.

Paul said, "I am become a fool in glorying; ye have compelled me: for I ought to have been commended of you: for in nothing am I behind the very chiefest apostles, though I be nothing" (2 Corinthians 12:11). Paul had a healthy view of himself in light of what he had done to the cause of Christ. He stated, "I be nothing." Paul knew who he was before when he was trying to destroy the church and after when he became a Christian.

When Paul knew that his life was ending he said,

"For I am now ready to be offered, and the time of my departure is at hand. I have fought a good fight, I have finished my course, I have kept the faith: Henceforth there is laid up for me a crown of righteousness, which the Lord, the righteous judge, shall give me at that day: and not to me only, but unto all them also that love his appearing" (2 Timothy 4:6–8).

Three times Paul asked God to remove his "thorn in the flesh" but God answered him: "My grace is sufficient for thee: for my strength is made perfect in weakness. Most gladly therefore will I rather glory in my infirmities, that the power of Christ may rest upon me" (2 Corinthians 12:9). My thorn in the flesh is Post Traumatic Stress Disorder (PTSD) and I get my strength from knowing that I am "Pleasing The Savior Daily."

Chapter 3

Survivals Guilt

Some gave all, all gave some, and some still give!

I told myself, "I survived Vietnam." Did I? Most do not understand that in Vietnam we talked about "going back to the world!" I had this fantasy that all would be well again when I got home to Linda and my family. That was not reality! I made it all the way home from the war in South Vietnam to face readjustment problems, flashbacks to combat situations, feelings of alienation, anger, depression, loneliness and the feeling of not wanting to get close to anyone anymore. When I became a Christian I was so thankful that my former life of being what I had been programmed to be was over. For a long time I was able to push it so far back into my mind that I actually forgot about it. I stayed busy with my church work. But, in 1978 it started to sneak back into my mind and it got worse as the years came. But I did not understand what was happening to me. I did not want to talk about it. I thought everyone was just like me – "normal!" I came to understand that I had violated what I had been taught all of my life, but in my thoughts and memories my guilt became acceptance.

Many of us who have survived Vietnam often ask, "Why did I survive when others more worthy than I did not?" "Why me, and not them?" "Why me Lord?" I learned that survival's guilt is a guilt-invoking symptom to Post Traumatic Stress Disorder. To many of the Vietnam veterans Post Traumatic Stress Disorder (PTSD) means "People That Survived Death." Survival's guilt is based on the harshest of realties. Only those who suffer with survival's guilt know the anguish and torment that it brings. It is based upon the actual death of a "brother" and the struggle of the surviving "brother" to live. Did the surviving "brother" compromise himself or some other "brother" in order to live? As a surviving "brother" could I have done something different so that my "brother" would not have died? What did I do wrong to cause this? The guilt of such an act invokes tremendous pain. This kind of guilt may end in self-destruction. What price must my heart pay to live and to love? Why is my heart numb? Where are my tears?

For years, I asked myself, "Why did Sergeant Jones have to die?" "Why was I the one who lived?" "Why wasn't it me?" Years later in my conversation with his only daughter, his brothers, and sisters they told me to, "Look at your life now and what it means. Your life is a life of giving and helping others." I went there to comfort, but I found comfort and compassion from those that I did not know.

I have seen the movie "Forrest Gump" through at least once. Linda was watching it while we were on vacation. When Forrest went back to get his "brothers," I became so involved in what was happening. I caught myself tensing up until finally when Forrest went back to get "Bubba" I had to leave the condo. I walked for over an hour telling myself over and over that it was alright to have the feelings that I was having. But then I began to tell myself if I had been there when Bradshaw and Moncrief were killed that maybe I could have changed it. But this is not true! Why was I lying to myself?

In my studies I have come to realize some things about guilt. Guilt does not bring happiness in the life of anyone. It breeds additional guilt. Guilt cannot be ignored. It must be dealt with or it will destroy one's mental stability and peace of mind.

Some try to blame others for their guilt. All of us remember that Adam tried to blame Eve and God for his sin. In addition, even Eve, tried to blame the serpent (Genesis 3:12, 13). The Bible teaches us that each one must bear his own guilt. No one else is responsible! The God of the Bible is no respecter of persons. Paul wrote,

> "But after thy hardness and impenitent heart treasurest up unto thyself wrath against the day of wrath and revelation of the righteous judgment of God; Who will render to every man according to his deeds: To them who by patient continuance in well

doing seek for glory and honour and immortality, eternal life: But unto them that are contentious, and do not obey the truth, but obey unrighteousness, indignation and wrath, Tribulation and anguish, upon every soul of man that doeth evil, of the Jew first, and also of the Gentile; But glory, honour, and peace, to every man that worketh good, to the Jew first, and also to the Gentile: For there is no respect of persons with God" (Romans 2:5–11).

Paul stated,

"For we must all appear before the judgment seat of Christ; that every one may receive the things *done* in *his* body, according to that he hath done, whether *it be* good or bad" (2 Corinthians 5:10).

There are those burdens that are so heavy that they consume all of our strength. I believe that there is no burden heavier than the burden of survivals guilt. Survivals guilt is a mixture of many emotions and thoughts which destroy one's inner peace. It is partly true and partly false.

David writes in Psalm 38:1-17 how that guilt caused him mental anguish and physical illness.

"O LORD, rebuke me not in thy wrath: neither chasten me in thy hot displeasure. For thine arrows stick fast in me, and thy hand presseth me sore. There is no soundness in my flesh because of thine anger; neither is there any rest in my bones because of my sin. For mine iniquities are gone over mine head: as an heavy burden they are too heavy for me. My wounds stink and are corrupt because of my foolishness. I am troubled; I am bowed down greatly; I go mourning all the day long. For my loins are filled with a loathsome disease: and there is no soundness in my flesh. I am feeble and sore broken: I have roared by reason of the disquietness of my heart. Lord, all my desire is before thee; and my groaning is not hid from thee. My heart panteth, my strength faileth me: as for the light of mine eyes, it also is gone from me. My lovers and my friends stand aloof from my sore; and my kinsmen stand afar off. They also that seek after my life lay snares for me: and they that seek my hurt speak mischievous things, and imagine deceits all the day long. But I, as a deaf man, heard not; and I was as a dumb man that openeth not his mouth. Thus I was as a man that heareth not, and in whose mouth are no reproofs. For in thee, O LORD, do I hope: thou wilt hear, O Lord my God. For I said, Hear me, lest otherwise they should rejoice over me: when my foot slippeth, they magnify themselves against me. For I am ready to halt, and my sorrow is continually before me" (Psalm 38:1–17).

In Psalm 51:1-4 David confesses his sins and he describes the relief that forgiveness brought.

"Have mercy upon me, O God, according to thy lovingkindness: according unto the multitude of thy tender mercies blot out my transgressions. Wash me throughly from mine iniquity, and cleanse me from my sin. For I acknowledge my transgressions: and my sin is ever before me. Against thee, thee only, have I sinned, and done this evil in thy sight: that thou mightest be justified when thou speakest, and be clear when thou judgest" (Psalm 51:1–4).

Psalm 51 is said to describe David after his sin with Bathsheba and arranging for the death of Uriah (Cf. 2 Samuel 11:1-12:15). In Psalm 32:1-4 David reveals that he knew that his suffering was from guilt.

"Blessed is he whose transgression is forgiven, whose sin is covered. Blessed is the man unto whom the LORD imputeth not iniquity, and in whose spirit there is no guile. When I kept silence, my bones waxed old through my roaring all the day long. For day and night thy hand was heavy upon me: my moisture is turned into the drought of summer. Selah" (Psalm 32:1–4).

In verses three and four, David thought that he had hidden his treacherous acts so well but what he had done was release his life into the pits of guilt. This guilt would pursue him "24/7" that is, when he was awake and when he was asleep. David gives great insight in Psalm 32:5 where he states, "I acknowledged my sin unto thee, and mine iniquity have I not hid. I said, I will confess my transgressions unto the LORD; and thou forgavest the iniquity of my sin." For years I "acknowledged my sin," survival's guilt, before God but did I "confess my transgressions unto the LORD?" Did God know that I was suffering from survivals guilt? Yes! Then why did He not do something? He had! But what had I done with this guilt? David's happiness came from him being forgiven by God!

How am I surviving survivals guilt? When serving in Vietnam my value system – my conscience – changed. I did what I was trained to do. I must admit it is still hard to look back at me in 1967 and 1968. I am not that person now, but how could I have been that person then? The TET (Vietnam's New Year) offensive of 1968 hardened my already hardened heart to the point that I enjoyed what I was doing as a combat soldier. I began surviving because my value system – my conscience – was changed just like Saul's was. But sometime after my obedience to the Gospel I began to ignore the cries of my survival's guilt and my conscience was again being hardened by my past. (1 Timothy 4:2). If I just stay busy, work harder, go back to school, or get another Bible study I will not have time to think about Vietnam.

I have studied the Bible "from cover to cover." I have undergraduate and graduate degrees in Bible. I even went back to college to earn a Master's degree in Counseling Psychology to help ME! What I failed to see was the correct biblical response to guilt. David got it right back in Psalm 32:5. I needed to "confess my transgressions unto the LORD." I needed to pray to God, my Father, and tell him ALL I did in Vietnam – ALL that happened in

1967 and 1968. Denial did not work. Concealing it did not work. Neither did becoming a "workaholic!" Paul said, "But by the grace of God I am what I am" (1 Corinthians 15:10). I do not need to condemn myself. I can live free from what happened in Vietnam.

I restudied 2 Corinthians 7:10. Paul says, "For godly sorrow worketh repentance to salvation not to be repented of: but the sorrow of the world worketh death." What I was now seeing was "godly sorrow" for my past. True repentance, a changing of my mind would result in a change of my direction toward God, my obedience to His commands about the past. I needed to deal with my survivals guilt and I did.

Have I erased February 7th, 1968 and all the other events from my mind? No. They are still there. I have "anniversary" dates and every year on those dates, I tearfully look back, but now I look back differently. I look back knowing that I have done all that my heavenly Father requires of me. I know, like Paul, that I cannot change any of those "anniversary" dates but I can continually "press toward the mark for the prize of the high calling of God in Christ Jesus (Philippians 3:14)." So that I will not forget Lowen's sacrifice for me, I still wear a stainless steel bracelet with his name and date of death on my wrist. I cannot forget Jesus' sacrifice for me, for I love Him with all of my heart, and with all of my soul, and with all of my mind and I love my neighbor (souls) as myself. (Matthew 22:37-39).

One of my favorite passages is 2 Peter 1:3-4 which says,

"According as his divine power hath given unto us all things that *pertain* unto life and godliness, through the knowledge of him that hath called us to glory and virtue: Whereby are given unto us exceeding great and precious promises: that by these ye might be partakers of the divine nature, having escaped the corruption that is in the world through lust."

God's word has all the answers that pertain to this life and to godly living. The knowledge to overcome all the things that pertain to living a godly life has been given.

> "And that from a child thou hast known the holy scriptures, which are able to make thee wise unto salvation through faith which is in Christ Jesus. All <u>scripture</u> is given by inspiration of God, and <u>is</u> <u>profitable for doctrine, for reproof, for correction,</u> <u>for instruction in righteousness</u>: That the man of God may be perfect, throughly furnished unto all good works" (2 Timothy 3:15–17).

It is true that the Scriptures teach us "doctrine" – What is right; "reproof" – What is not right; "correction" – How to get right; and "instruction" – How to stay right. God has furnished us with everything we need in the "scriptures."

My thorn in the flesh is Post Traumatic Stress Disorder (PTSD) and PTSD means many things to many people but to me it has come to mean "Pleasing The Savior Daily."

Chapter 4

Depression

The wise man Solomon said, "Heaviness in the heart of man maketh it stoop: but a good word maketh it glad." (Proverbs 12:25). The Hebrew word for "heaviness" is *dâ'agah* which means, "1 anxiety, anxious care, care" (Strong H1674). The word "stoop" is from the Hebrew word *shachah* which means "1 to bow down. 1A (Qal) to bow down. 1B (Hiphil) to depress (fig). 1C (Hithpael). 1C1 to bow down, prostrate oneself. 1C1A before superior in homage. 1C1B before God in worship. 1C1C before false gods. 1C1D before angel" (Strong, H7812). When the word is used in the imperfect, hiphil, which means an uncompleted condition; that is to say a depressed condition that is uncompleted; it is a continual state of depression, therefore the one who is depressed is getting lower and lower! The person becomes depressed or dejected. As a Christian, why did I get so depressed? Did you notice that Solomon speaks about "in the heart?" (Strong H3820).

There are many signs of a person's suffering from Post Traumatic Stress Disorder depression. These may include an inability to concentrate, moving more slowly than normal, pessimism, lethargy, agitation, anxiety, fears, feelings of guilt, hopelessness, apathy, living in the past, feeling useless, low self-esteem, a negative view of the world and one's future. Depression can lead to substance abuse and thoughts of suicide or an attempt of suicide. A depressed person loses perspective. The way that they look at their life, their job, and their family is out of focus. We have a distortion about ourselves, life, and God. We become a negative thinking person about life.

Many Vietnam veterans who are suffering from Post Traumatic Stress Disorder have a "death wish." To illustrate this point, one veteran stated that when driving and someone pulled out in front of him that he does not try to slow down. He stated, "That would not be suicide, it would be an accident."

It is estimated that over 15% of those who are depressed will commit suicide. The disorders of depression affect over 18 million Americans each year. It is estimated that by 2020 depression will be the second largest killer after heart disease. It should also be noted that studies have shown that depression contributes to coronary heart disease. This is a double problem for the Vietnam veteran because Agent Orange is a cause of coronary heart disease.

The Vietnam veteran who is suffering from Post Traumatic Stress Disorder will have times of depression and will manifest many of the signs listed above. Solomon said in Proverbs 17:22, "A merry heart doeth good like a medicine: but a broken spirit drieth the bones." What could I do about my "broken spirit?" Again, Solomon refers to the "heart."

There are Bible people who became depressed. Moses stated,

> "I am not able to bear all this people alone, because it is too heavy for me. And if thou deal thus with me, kill me, I pray thee, out of hand, if I have found favour in thy sight; and let me not see my wretchedness" (Numbers 11:14-15).

Moses faced a crisis! He preferred death rather than to continue his life. Moses' words contained discontent, despair, and seeds of rebellion. Moses' focus is on his own misery. But Moses was not alone!

Samuel stated,

> "But the Spirit of the LORD departed from Saul, and an evil spirit from the LORD troubled him. And Saul's servants said unto him, Behold now, an evil spirit from God troubleth thee. Let our lord now command thy servants, which are before thee, to seek out a man, who is a cunning player on an harp: and it shall come to pass, when the evil spirit

from God is upon thee, that he shall play with his hand, and thou shalt be well. And Saul said unto his servants, Provide me now a man that can play well, and bring him to me. Then answered one of the servants, and said, Behold, I have seen a son of Jesse the Bethlehemite, that is cunning in playing, and a mighty valiant man, and a man of war, and prudent in matters, and a comely person, and the LORD is with him. Wherefore Saul sent messengers unto Jesse, and said, Send me David thy son, which is with the sheep. And Jesse took an ass laden with bread, and a bottle of wine, and a kid, and sent them by David his son unto Saul. And David came to Saul, and stood before him: and he loved him greatly; and he became his armourbearer. And Saul sent to Jesse, saying, Let David, I pray thee, stand before me; for he hath found favour in my sight. And it came to pass, when the evil spirit from God was upon Saul, that David took an harp, and played with his hand: so Saul was refreshed, and was well, and the evil spirit departed from him" (1 Samuel 16:14-23).

As I read this passage, I see Saul deteriorating mentally. Whatever the "evil spirit" was, it invaded the mind of Saul. Do we find here one of the causes of depression? Do we find one of the means to aid the one depressed?

There are other Biblical people who were depressed: Elijah in 1 Kings 19:1-18; David in Psalms 31:9-16; Jeremiah in Jeremiah 15:10; 20:14-18; and Job in Job 10:1.

As a Christian how could I deal with depression? I had studied both the Bible and counseling psychology. I needed to bring those two together, because the Bible says that God "hath given unto us all things that pertain to life and godliness, through the knowledge of Him that hath called us to glory and virtue" (2 Peter 1:3).

43

Arthur Freeman stated, "The basic premise of the cognitive-behavioral therapy (CBT) model is that there is an essential interaction between the way individuals feel and behave and the way in which they construe their world, themselves, and the prospect for their future" (Freeman p. 19). The goal is to help uncover dysfunctional and irrational thinking, to reality-test thinking behavior, and to build more adaptive functional techniques for responding to one's thought patterns. Is this the "miracle cure" for depression that is related to Post Traumatic Stress Disorder? No! This type of therapy helps us to develop better coping strategies to deal with life. This is my way of bringing the Bible and counseling psychology together. The strategies help us to focus on the negative distortions. For example, "If I had been there instead of being on R&R (Rest and Relaxation), he would not have been killed." This is a distortion of the truth! The source of our distortions is irrational belief systems. My conflict was not with what the Bible said but with those irrational belief systems that I had formed in my mind and accepted. Because of not telling myself the truth, I was in and out of a depressed state. How could I escape depression?

Saul used music. I taught myself how to play the guitar. But I caught myself singing the "sad" songs. That did not help my situation. I even wrote a song about my tour in Vietnam. It is included in this book. My coping strategy had not been developed at that time.

Then, I began to look again at what the Bible said about "life." In Galatians 5:22 the phrase "the fruit of the spirit" is stated. As I studied this passage I concluded that this was not the Holy Spirit, but it was my inner spirit, that which was given to me by God. That the context of the passage was showing the fleshly man verses the spiritual man. I looked at the words that were used, "love, joy, peace, longsuffering, gentleness, goodness, faith, meekness, temperance..." (Galatians 5:22-23). So the Bible was telling me that "faith" is part of the fruit of my inner spirit. How am I to obtain this "faith?" I knew the Biblical answer to that question. "So then faith cometh by hearing, and hearing by the word of God" (Romans 10:17). Therefore I concluded if I hear what God is saying then my inner spirit will bear the fruit of faith. But not only faith, but all of the terms that are used in Galatians 5:22-23 because the word "fruit" is singular. I can have all of those by listening to what God has said in His Word. In John 16:33 Jesus told His apostles that they would have peace. Paul was chosen to be an apostle AFTER he made havoc of the church! In some of His last words Jesus stated in Revelation 22:14 that those who "do His commandments" are blessed. Therefore, I needed to work on my irrational belief systems. I needed to let the Bible tell me the truth and apply that truth to my past and present in order to overcome depression.

Peter said, "Casting all your care upon Him; for He careth for you" (1 Peter 5:7). When I became depressed my mind (heart) became an anxious mind, but God still cared for me. The care that God provides is a continuous caring. When my depressed mind (heart) was filled with hopelessness, God provided me with hope. "In hope of eternal life, which God, that cannot lie, promised before the world began" (Titus 1:2).

My depressed confused mind (heart) was not from God "For God is not the author of confusion…" (1 Corinthians 14:33). When I felt depressed I knew that it was not from God. I knew that I did not have God (His Word) in my mind. My mind was on what had happened in Vietnam in 1967 and 1968. My mind was on my past!

In Philippians 4:13, Paul said, "I can do all things through Christ which strengtheneth me." "I can" [as opposed to I cannot, an attitude of "I can" has the power to cope with, is competent] "do all things" [as fitting the context] "through Christ" [who said, ". . . He that abideth in me, and I in him, the same bringeth forth much fruit: for without me you can do nothing" (John 14:5)] "which strenghteneth me" [he empowers, trains, encourages, etc.]. There were many Biblical truths that kept coming to my mind. "For as he thinketh in his heart, so is he…. (Proverbs 23:7)." Remember earlier I mentioned that Solomon spoke of "the heart" in Proverbs 12:25 and 17:22. I concluded I am what I think!

"And he saith unto them, Are ye so without understanding also? Do ye not <u>perceive</u>, that whatsoever thing from without entereth into the man, it cannot defile him; Because it entereth not into his heart, but into the belly, and goeth out into the draught, purging all meats? And he said, That which cometh out of the man, that defileth the man. For from within, out of the heart of men, proceed evil thoughts, adulteries, fornications, murders, Thefts, covetousness, wickedness, deceit, lasciviousness, an evil eye, blasphemy, pride, foolishness: <u>All these evil things come from within,</u> and defile the man" (Mark 7:18–23).

I understood Jesus to teach that it was not what was on the outside that defiles the man but what proceeds from his heart (mind). What was in my heart? (See also Matthew 12:35–37). Good things were to proceed from a good heart but evil things from an evil heart.

My coping strategy to deal with my life was simple. I would tell myself that it was okay for me to remember the events of Vietnam in 1967 and 1968, but that I was not going to allow them to rob me of the "fruit of my spirit (my inner spirit, my inner me). I knew that at anytime something or someone could remind me of my Vietnam experience, but I also knew that I had to deal with it and go on with my life. I concluded that if I continued in a depressed state that I would not be able to be "Pleasing The Savior Daily."

I talk to myself! Do you? Earlier I mentioned about watching "Forrest Gump." Yes, I was reminded of Vietnam 1967 and 1968. But, I told myself the truth. I do not know if the situation would have been any different if I had been there and telling myself that it would, is a lie. "But if" does not help the person who is suffering from Post Traumatic Stress Disorder depression!

The Bible tells us upon what our thoughts are to be.

> "Finally, brethren, <u>whatsoever things are true,</u> whatsoever things *are* <u>honest</u>, whatsoever things *are* <u>just</u>, whatsoever things *are* <u>pure</u>, whatsoever things *are* <u>lovely</u>, whatsoever things *are* <u>of good report</u>; <u>if *there be* any virtue, and if *there be* any praise, think on these things</u>" (Philippians 4:8).

Even though Paul experienced depression, he knew where to keep his thoughts!

Paul asked God three times to remove his "thorn in the flesh" but God said to Paul, "My grace is sufficient for thee: for my strength is made perfect in weakness. Most gladly therefore will I rather glory in my infirmities, that the power of Christ may rest upon me" (2 Corinthians 12:9). Paul suffered from his "thorn in the flesh" for the rest of his life but he did not let a lack of faith (trust and obey) destroy him with depression.

I listened to Paul repeatedly when he said,

> "Not that I speak in respect of want: for I have learned, in whatsoever state I am, *therewith* to be content. I know both how to be abased, and I know how to abound: everywhere and in all things I am instructed both to be full and to be hungry, both to abound and to suffer need. I can do all things through Christ which strengtheneth me" (Philippians 4:11-13).

Paul's total trust in God enabled him to be "...more than conquerors through Him that loved us" (Romans 8:37).

Do I still have times of depression that are brought about because of my Vietnam experience? Yes, but the Bible has the answer on how to deal with it. My thorn in the flesh is Post Traumatic Stress Disorder (PTSD) and I can do what I need to do to live a faithful Christian life, "Pleasing The Savior Daily."

Chapter 5

Withdrawn Behavior

What is considered withdrawn behavior? This behavior is marked by isolation, avoidance, and silence. It occurs when one cannot relate to another individual. Friends are few in number. That is why being in counseling with other Vietnam veterans is vital. Many Vietnam veterans, after finding a counseling group, find that they are "normal" because they are like everyone in the group. If the person suffering is married, then his marriage is in jeopardy. Many combat veterans have become preoccupied with memories of things that happened "in Nam." Because of the preoccupation of those memories difficulties in relating one's thoughts or any feeling of anger or sadness is not shared with anyone. Why? Because when one of them tries no one wants to listen, therefore one feels rejected. One's mind is saying, "I just want to be alone and left alone." One just shuts "everyone out." The veteran who is suffering from Post Traumatic Stress Disorder thinks that he is doing "everybody" a favor by withdrawing. But this is not so! At times I felt like I was living in two worlds. There were times that I felt like an old man trapped in a young man's body. Again I was lying to myself so that I would not have to deal with my irrational belief system.

How can we overcome isolation? Isolation can be overcome by focusing. As a Christian my focus should be on "Pleasing The Savior Daily." But there are those times that I just want to be alone. It is during those times that I am able just to think. I try not to think of Vietnam, but I do think of all the good men with whom I served. This is awkward meditation because I only remember those with whom I served in Vietnam.

Once while I was away from my platoon they were sent on a mission. Our Lieutenant was given the directions that the helicopters would make their approach. Members of the platoon were told that it would be a "hot LZ" (incoming fire at the landing zone). The point man and squad leader were told the direction that they were to go when they exited the helicopter. The squad leader told the point man that when he tapped him on the back that he was to exit the helicopter. The wind shifted while they were in the air to the LZ (landing zone). This meant that the directions changed. The squad leader tapped the point man on the back to tell him the new directions, but the point man jumped out of the helicopter. The point man should have been given his "wings" for that jump. He jumped over twenty-five feet into a rice paddy. They had to set up a perimeter and remove him from the mud. I understood that only his head stuck out of the mud. Yes, we did have good memories, times of laughter, and some fun.

David wrote, "Out of the depths have I cried unto thee, O LORD" (Psalm 130:1). Here David is speaking from the depths of despair. The language resembles the language in Psalm 69:2 and 14 where David says,

> "I sink in deep mire, where *there is* no standing: I am come into deep waters, where the floods overflow me...Deliver me out of the mire, and let me not sink: Let me be delivered from them that hate me, and out of the deep waters."

David states his cause for his despair. "If thou, LORD, shouldest mark iniquities, O Lord, who shall stand? But there is forgiveness with thee, That thou mayest be feared" (Psalm 130:3-4). What caused this despair was what David personally did and what his people had done. David shows his impatience as he waits on the LORD to help. "I wait for the LORD, my soul doth wait, And in His word do I hope . My soul waiteth for the Lord More than they hat watch for the morning: I say, more than they that watch for the morning" (Psalm 130:4-5). In these verses David expresses his deep longing for the LORD to rescue him from his despair. David's waiting is not hopeless. Why? David had placed his trust in the Word of God. Here was David's hope for his despair.

God said that, "It is not good that the man should be alone" (Genesis 2:18). God wanted man to have a "help meet." The point I want to make from this is that God did not want man to be by himself. That man needed someone with whom he could talk.

My room became "my safe place." Was I withdrawing to "my room" because I was discontented? How could Paul write?

> "Not that I speak in respect of want: for I have learned, in whatsoever state I am, therewith to be content. I know both how to be abased, and I know how to abound: every where and in all things I am instructed both to be full and to be hungry, both to abound and to suffer need" (Philippians 4:11–12).

How could he be content being in a prison cell? Paul wrote, "I have learned" that contentment and happiness are not dependent on external circumstances, but on inner qualities of the heart. I see the pattern now, but I did not see it when I was struggling with Post Traumatic Stress Disorder and withdrew to "my room."

I remembered what Peter had written. "According as his divine power hath given unto us all things that pertain unto life and godliness, through the knowledge of him that hath called us to glory and virtue" (2 Peter 1:3). Paul wrote, "But godliness with contentment is great gain" (1 Timothy 6:6). How does godliness come? It comes through the knowledge of the Christ who has called us by the gospel. Here again the pattern is being seen. The Bible has the answers but my irrational belief system was interfering with all that I had learned. My focus was not correct. I kept focusing on the problems that I was having with my irrational belief system instead of focusing on the knowledge that I had obtained from studying the Bible. My faulty thinking had put me in despair. I withdrew to "my room," thinking that there was no hope of my ever finding the correct answers to my Vietnam experience. No hope of finally being at peace with the inner me! But, I was wrong.

Isaiah wrote, " Come now, and let us reason together, saith the LORD: Though your sins be as scarlet, they shall be as white as snow; Though they be red like crimson, they shall be as wool" (Isaiah 1:18). The time for reason had come. I could not find a solution using my knowledge of God's Word and my irrational belief system. Once I reasoned this out there was no need for me to withdraw, to isolate myself from anyone. I no longer was being preoccupied with my memories of Vietnam.

A number of the Vietnam Veterans of Bartow County (Cartersville, Georgia) went to the Vet Center in Atlanta for help. We met with the counselor who was also a Vietnam Veteran. He began to meet with us in Cartersville every week. This was 1997 and he still meets with veterans and their spouses. "The Group" helped me to understand that there were others like me. That is "normal!" "The Group" was a great help in encouraging us not to withdraw within ourselves because there were others who were "normal." Many who came to the group expressed that they were glad to find some people who were "normal." "The Group" became a means to social activity for those who attended and also for their families.

Do I still withdraw, isolated myself from others? Yes! But it is not to be preoccupied with Vietnam memories. It is a time to pray, think and study. It is also a time to be refreshed. In "my room" when I withdraw, I tell myself the truth. I replace my irrational beliefs with the truth of God's Word.

My wife Linda knows if I am having problems. She asked, "Are you okay?" Here is my "help meet." God knew that man was not to be alone. I replied, "Yes, I am doing fine." Do you know what "fine" means? Fine means "Feelings Inside Not Expressed." If I wanted to express how I was doing, she was there to listen and give advice. But if I did not want to express my feelings because I had not thought them through, she understood. I know that when I am ready I have someone to help me. I have truly been blessed with such a wonderful woman. I now know that the stress that I placed on my family was enormous.

Veterans that suffer from Post Traumatic Stress Disorder need to be in counseling. It is my suggestion that they get individual counseling first and then go into a group where veterans are being counseled. As I have stated, we who suffer from Post Traumatic Stress Disorder are "normal." In "The Group" we had a new

Vietnam veteran who had been in individual counseling join us. His wife also went to "The Wives' Group." She later related her first session. She stated that she sat there in her chair and listen to all of the other wives describe "her husband." How could that be? Veterans that suffer from Post Traumatic Stress Disorder are "normal." They are all alike!

The Psalmist said, "Why standest thou afar off, O LORD? *Why* hidest thou *thyself* in times of trouble?" (Psalm 10:1). My thorn in the flesh is Post Traumatic Stress Disorder (PTSD) and my solution for overcoming my withdrawal behavior was to be "Pleasing The Savior Daily."

Chapter 6

Inner Rage

There is an inner rage within the mind of the combat veteran. Many of us feel like no one understands us when we try to express this inner rage. Our response to them is simply, "you don't understand" or "you will not understand." I thought that if I told everything that I had done in Vietnam that those who were listening would think that they were horrible crimes and therefore, I was a horrible person. But, this was another lie I was telling myself. Most people would conclude that they were actions that were committed because they were the only means of surviving in war.

It was very difficult to come to the truth that there were those who wanted to understand. Linda wanted to understand the man she waited for and married. But, I was not ready to tell the one that helped me make it through Vietnam all that I had done.

I was at the church building repairing one of the tanks on a toilet in the woman's bathroom. The Tabitha class was meeting on that day. The young girls came by making jokes about my being in the "women's bathroom." It was funny! But, one of the young girls came to the door of the bathroom and screamed. It was not funny. The scream carried me back to Vietnam. I ran after her because I thought something was wrong. After coming to myself, I proceeded to tell this little girl the effect her scream had on me. My granddaughter ran and got the woman in charge and she talked to me in such a way that I calmed down. I left the building and the next thing I remembered I was entering the front door of our house. I was thinking "I know that Linda will understand." I was embarrassed and ashamed of what I had done to that young girl. The rage within me was seen by her, my granddaughter, and those who were at the Tabitha class. That night the girl's grandfather comforted his granddaughter and then he comforted me. This was one of the turning points in my wanting to find a solution for my Post Traumatic Stress Disorder. Even to this day, every time I see this grandfather he hugs me and tells me that he loves me!

This inner rage is a frightening thing because it can become violent. I am so thankful that I never became violent. But I know that there were times that my wife and my children saw someone that they did not know. There were times that my behavior must have been very frightening to them. I was ashamed of how I reacted when things did not go the way I thought they should. I tried to learn from each of these episodes. However, there were times that I forgot all that I had learned. This struggle became a fight for my spiritual survival. How can I as a Christian act that way?

Moses wrote,

> "But unto Cain and to his offering he had not respect. And Cain was very wroth, and his countenance fell. And the LORD said unto Cain, Why art thou wroth? and why is thy countenance fallen? If thou doest well, shalt thou not be accepted? and if thou doest not well, sin lieth at the door. And unto thee *shall be* his desire, and thou shalt rule over him. And Cain talked with Abel his brother: and it came to pass, when they were in the field, that Cain rose up against Abel his brother, and slew him" (Genesis 4:5-8).

The Hebrew word here for "wroth" means, "1 to be hot, furious, burn, become angry, be kindled. 1A (Qal) to burn, kindle (anger). 1B (Niphal) to be angry with, be incensed. 1C (Hiphil) to burn, kindle. 1D (Hithpael) to heat oneself in vexation" (Strong H2734). I noted that Moses said, "Very wroth." The wise man Solomon wrote, "He that hath no rule over his own spirit Is like a city that is broken down, and without walls (Proverbs 25:28)." The Hebrew word here for "rule," means, "1 restraint, control" (Strong H4623). The Hebrew word for "broken down" has the meaning "to break out (violently) upon...to break over (limits), increase...to use violence...to burst open..." (Strong H6555). At times I felt defenseless and out of control. There seemed to be no walls to protect me.

In Galatians 5:22-23, within Paul's list of the "fruit (singular) of the spirit (my inner spirit)" the word "temperance" is given. The Greek word εγκρατεια means, "self-control (the virtue of one who masters his desires and passions, esp. his sensual appetites)" (Strong G1466). How could I master "temperance" (self-control)? Paul had already given the answer. Since "faith" is referred to as a part of the "fruit of the spirit" and this "faith" comes through the word of God (Romans 10:17), I concluded, that God has given me the answer to this rage within me.

I had repressed the rage that I had within me and felt no obligation to deal with it. I told myself that I had every right to feel the way I did because of the way I was trained and treated when I return to the United States of America. My training in the Army equated rage with masculine identity in the performance of military duty. My inner self was filled with resentment and rage. I realized that the inner rage within me was stored up anger. As I tried to analyze the situation with the young girl, I began to see how all of the symptoms of Post Traumatic Stress Disorder worked together. The young girl's scream sent me back to Vietnam. Certain sounds trigger my thoughts back to Vietnam. There are sounds you never forget.

Some time after the event with the young girl at church some of the church members went out to eat. I had only eaten at this place one time. When Linda and I walked in the hostess popped a balloon. I knew that I was not in Vietnam but my thoughts were. We had been ambushed. But this is not reality! I grabbed for the wall, it was real! Linda later said she knew immediately the effect it would have on me and grabbed my arm. The hostess thought I was having a heart attack. Linda explained to her. The young hostess apologized. One of the members later told me that they would never forget the look I had on my face. No, I did not leave the restaurant because of being embarrassed. Vietnam was not going to control me anymore.

It was during that time that I had already decided that I did not die in Vietnam and that I was not going to allow the symptoms of Post Traumatic Stress Disorder to destroy me. I learned that I was in control of me. I knew that the only way that I could "make the best" of my life was to deal with these fears. I studied the book of 1 John and found my answers.

> "But whoso keepeth his word, in him verily is the love of God perfected: hereby know we that we are in him…No man hath seen God at any time. If we love one another, God dwelleth in us, and his love is perfected in us…Herein is our love made perfect, that we may have boldness in the day of judgment: because as he is, so are we in this world. There is no fear in love; but perfect love casteth out fear: because fear hath torment. He that feareth is not made perfect in love" (1 John 2:5; 4:12, 17–18).

If I continued to keep God's word then the love of God would be perfected and I could know that I was "in Him." Why have the fears about falling back to the man of 1967 and 1968? The key was to "continue to keep" (keep on keeping on) God's word. If I love my fellow man as God has so instructed, then God's love would be perfected in me. Since this love is perfected by continuing in God's word and loving my fellow man it would continue to cast out fear. Perfect love continues to cast out anxiety/fear! If I continue in anxiety/fear then my love is not perfected.

The Bible says,

> "Wherefore let him that thinketh he standeth take heed lest he fall. There hath no temptation taken you but such as is common to man: but God is faithful, who will not suffer you to be tempted above that ye are able; but will with the temptation also make a way to escape, that ye may be able to bear it" (1 Corinthians 10:12-13).

My thorn in the flesh is Post Traumatic Stress Disorder (PTSD) and I found my way to escape, "Pleasing The Savior Daily!"

Chapter 7

Avoidance of Feelings

In sixteen weeks of infantry training, I was prepared to go to Vietnam. As I looked back over those training days I came to realized that I was taught not to look at the Vietnamese as people. During training they were labeled as "gooks, dinks, and VC (Viet Cong)." This was a way to dehumanize the Vietnamese as a person. We even dehumanized ourselves by referring to ourselves as "grunts." Why were we taught this? I concluded it was a way to harden our minds (hearts) against having feelings for another and even for one's self. This was re-enforced in Vietnam. Once a sick "scout dog" was dusted off while wounded soldiers waited on the next helicopter. Why? It took a lot of money to train a dog and we understood that, then. We were just a number according to some of those in Washington D.C. and to those who were demonstrating we were "baby killers." I felt that the only way I could protect myself was to harden an already hardened heart.

On February 7th, 1968, Sergeant Jones was killed when he stood up and motioned for me to get down. During the whole time that we were trying to get to him I was responding as a soldier should. I radioed the LT and told him that Sergeant Jones was hit. We were told to pull back. We were not going to leave him! We laid down fire so that the medic and the others could get to him from a different angle. Later when we took his body back to where we had been dug in, I became very emotional. I was trained to be a soldier but I was brought up by my mother to show love and compassion for others. This love and compassion brought pain to my mind (heart). I did not want to hurt nor cry anymore! I began to avoid my feelings. I was numb! It took me over fifty days to relate the events of February 7th, 1968 to Linda and my mother.

I had come to believe that if I allowed myself to show love and compassion for others as my mother taught me, that I was going to lose control of myself. This was and is a lie! But it worked for me until I came home. "Back in the world" I would love and show compassion because I was told to put my past behind me and get on with my life. This was fantasy! The only ones I showed love and compassion to were Linda, and our immediate families. This was my "squad." But even with them it was hard to let myself fully get attached because I knew someday they would die. I did not want to hurt anymore!

Linda and I obeyed the gospel of Christ on September 24th, 1970. Our lives changed. I felt like a new person. Why? "Therefore if any man be in Christ, he is a new creature: old things are passed away; behold, all things are become new" (2 Corinthians 5:17). I allowed myself to get close to members of the church. I began to experience feelings of love and compassion. It was a giving and receiving experience. But, it was depressing when some of them would move away. The hurt that I did not want to feel anymore came back when any of them died. I struggled within myself. But I was learning that the members of the church and my classmates at the Memphis School of Preaching were concerned about my spiritual life like my Vietnam "brothers" had been about my physical life.

David said, "But thou, O Lord, art a God full of compassion and gracious, longsuffering, and plenteous in mercy and truth. (Psalm 86:15). He would go on in verse sixteen and ask God to "give thy strength unto thy servant." David stated that, "The LORD is gracious, and full of compassion; slow to anger, and of great mercy. The LORD is good to all: and his tender mercies are over all his works" (Psalm 145:8-9). Peter stated that God "hath given unto us all things that pertain unto life and godliness, through the knowledge of him that hath called us to glory and virtue" (2 Peter 1:3).

Jesus was often moved with compassion. Matthew states, "But when he saw the multitude, he was moved with compassion on them, because they fainted, and were scattered abroad, as sheep having no shepherd" (Matthew 9:36). Jesus is our example! The shepherd cared for his sheep. Here was my inner conflict. Now that I am a Christian how could I care, have compassion, and love my fellow man? My mind (heart) had changed. Like David, I needed the strength that only God could give. My Vietnam heart and my

Christian heart were in the biggest battle that I had ever fought. My Christian heart wanted to love and have compassion but my Vietnam heart did not want to hurt, nor cry anymore. Peter wrote, "Finally, be ye all of one mind, having compassion one for another, love as brethren, be pitiful, be courteous" (1 Peter 3:8). John stated, "But whoso hath this world's good, and seeth his brother have need, and shutteth up his bowels of compassion from him, how dwelleth the love of God in him?" (1 John 3:17).

What would Paul do? When I re-studied Paul's life, I found my answer! As I read and searched I found all of those passages where Paul wrote about what "we" and "us" had "in Christ." Paul was not a Christian when he tried to destroy the Lord's church. Paul speaks of a battle going on in the life of a Christian. This battle is a spiritual battle between the "flesh" and "the spirit" (the inner self). I took a closer look at some of the passages that used the word "spirit (the inner man)" and "Spirit." Some of those that had "Spirit" should have "spirit (the inner man)."

Paul had never been to the church in Rome but he wrote to them. He stated,

> "There is <u>therefore now no condemnation to them which are in Christ Jesus, who walk not after the flesh, but after the spirit</u>. For the law of the spirit of life in Christ Jesus hath made me free from the law of sin and death. For what the law could not do, in that it was weak through the flesh, God sending his own Son in the likeness of sinful flesh, and for sin, condemned sin in the flesh: That the righteousness of the law might be fulfilled in us, who walk not after the flesh, but after the spirit. <u>For they that are after the flesh do mind the things of the flesh; but they that are after the spirit the things of the spirit.</u> For to be carnally minded is death; but to be spiritually minded is life and peace. Because the carnal mind is enmity against God: for it is not subject to the law of God, neither indeed can be. So then they that are in the flesh cannot please God.

But ye are not in the flesh, but in the spirit, if so be that the Spirit of God dwell in you. <u>Now if any man have not the spirit of Christ, he is none of his</u>. And if Christ be in you, the body is dead because of sin; <u>but the spirit is life because of righteousness</u>" (Romans 8:1–10).

Here is the battle that I was fighting. It is a battle between the fleshly man and the spiritual man. Listen to what Paul had stated.

> "<u>For I delight in the law of God after the inward man:</u> But I see <u>another law in my members, warring against the law of my mind,</u> and bringing me into captivity to the law of sin which is in my members. O wretched man that I am! who shall deliver me from the body of this death? I thank God through Jesus Christ our Lord. So then with the mind I myself serve the law of God; but with the flesh the law of sin" (Romans 7:22–25).

There was a war going on in my mind. Listen to Paul! "O wretched man that I am! who shall deliver me from the body of this death?" (Romans 7:24). The trials and toils of Vietnam would not go away. Therefore, I had a choice. Who is going to win this war? I had to learn, yes learn, how to show compassion and love. Paul said, "Not that I speak in respect of want: <u>for I have learned</u>, in whatsoever state I am, therewith to be content" (Philippians 4:11). Sometimes I felt like those who are spoken of in 2 Timothy 3:7. "Ever learning, and never able to come to the knowledge of the truth." Paul gives a description of God's word in Hebrews 4:12.

> "For <u>the word of God </u>is quick, and powerful, and sharper than any twoedged sword, piercing even to the dividing asunder of soul and spirit, and of the joints and marrow, and <u>is a discerner of the thoughts and intents of the heart</u>."

Paul describes what can be done with the mind when one applies God's word.

"I beseech you therefore, brethren, by the mercies of God, that ye present your bodies a living sacrifice, holy, acceptable unto God, which is your reasonable service. And be not conformed to this world: but be ye transformed by the renewing of your mind, that ye may prove what is that good, and acceptable, and perfect, will of God" (Romans 12:1-2)

Isaiah said,

"Let the wicked forsake his way, and the unrighteous man his thoughts: and let him return unto the LORD, and he will have mercy upon him; and to our God, for he will abundantly pardon. For my thoughts are not your thoughts, neither are your ways my ways, saith the LORD. For as the heavens are higher than the earth, so are my ways higher than your ways, and my thoughts than your thoughts" (Isaiah 55:7–9).

I knew that the mind was a powerful tool if it was guided by the word of God, but if it was not, it could lead me down a path that I did not want to go. I was to have "a pure conscience" (1 Timothy 3:9). At times I felt like my conscience had been, "seared with a hot iron" (1 Timothy 4:2). There is hope for all of us who suffer with Post Traumatic Stress Disorder. "Let us draw near with a true heart in full assurance of faith, having our hearts sprinkled from an evil conscience, and our bodies washed with pure water" (Hebrews 10:22). I wanted to be able to have compassion and to love as the Bible says. My thorn in the flesh is Post Traumatic Stress Disorder (PTSD) and I chose with the mind (heart) to serve God by "Pleasing The Savior Daily."

Chapter 8

Anger

When I returned to "the world" on September 1st, 1968, I had gotten all cleaned up, given new clothing, and received all the back pay the Army owed me. Here I sat in my "Class A's" with the medals, the ribbons, the blue infantry rope, and my sergeant strips being informed that we probably should not wear the uniform to the airport for our own protection. Do what? This was the uniform of the United States Army! I had fought for my country and I had the right to wear this uniform wherever and whenever I wanted as long as it was in accordance with the rules and regulations of the United States Army. Five of us skipped the T-bone steak dinner. We rented a taxi and went to the airport in our "Class A's!" We did not encounter any problems at the airport. I felt "anger."

While at the airport I left to call my family to tell them that I was in the USA, even though I was in California! I told them that I would land in Atlanta, Georgia the next day around 9 AM. However, because of fog, we went to Jacksonville, Florida first. When I returned to be with "my brothers" they were ordering a drink. I ordered a drink. Then I was asked for by ID. I whipped out my Army ID card and the waitress smiled and said, "You are too young to drink in California." My friend Sergeant Holley said, "Also bring me what he ordered." She stated that she would bring him the drink but then she said, "If I see him drinking it I will have to take it away from him." But I smiled and said, "Bring me a Coke." Anger! Too young to drink but not too young to spend a year fighting in Vietnam!

I kept my anger under control while I finished my time at Fort Benning Georgia. I worked on the S 3 Training Committee as their clerk. We taught a refresher course for those who were going overseas. If you were in Fort Benning and going outside the USA, you had to come through this training committee. Some of those who came through were people with whom I had gone through Basic Training. They and others informed me that they did not want to go to Vietnam. I stated that I went and did my duty. Who do "they think they are?" I felt "anger."

Why was I so angry? I was angry because Washington would not let us win the war. I was angry because I was not given a welcome home. I was angry because the way I was treated by the system. I was angry because veteran's organization did not want me to join. I was angry because when I complained about my health issues I felt like they thought I was lying. I was angry because no one, except my wife, knew I was having problems. I was angry because it seemed no one cared about us. I became even angrier when I was told that "we" lost the war in Vietnam. "We" never lost a battle in Vietnam. My anger is stirred when I read an obituary that says that the deceased was a "veteran of the Korean or Vietnam Conflict." They were "WARS!" See my anger? My angriest moment came when a retired Army sergeant told me that "Vietnam was not a war." Vietnam was not like any other war that the USA had fought that's for sure. Our hands were tied! Even now I can "rant and rave" about what we were not allowed to do! But, the Vietnam War is now over except in the minds of those who fought there. We were there last night!

What was I to do with this angry conscience? I tried to deal with it as it occurred. A lot of my anger was self inflicted by my own irrational belief system. Some people knew what buttons to push to put me and other Vietnam veterans on the defensive. I came to the conclusion that when I allowed anyone to "rile me up" they were in control of my life. I also understood that when I allowed my irrational belief system to "kick in" I could "rile me up" on the inside and it would manifest itself on the outside. To answer the question above: I was going to re-train my angry conscience!

Paul wrote, "Let all bitterness, and wrath, and anger, and clamour, and evil speaking, be put away from you, with all malice" (Ephesians 4:31). When I looked at this verse I knew that I have to find a solution to my problem. Paul, writing by inspiration was not making a suggestion; he was commanding the Christian to put these things away. "Bitterness" comes from the Greek word πικρια, which means "bitter hatred" (Strong G4088). "Wrath" comes from the Greek word θυμος which means, "passion anger, heat, anger forthwith boiling up; and soon subsiding again" (Strong G2372). The Greek for anger is οργη and means, "anger, the natural disposition, temper, character…movement or agitation of the soul, impulse, desire, any violent emotion…anger, wrath, indignation…." (Strong G3709). The wise man Solomon said, "He that is slow to anger is better than the mighty; And he that ruleth his spirit than he that taketh a city" (Proverbs 16:32). When I am angry am I ruling my spirit (the inner man)? "Be not hasty in thy spirit to be angry: for anger resteth in the bosom of fools" (Ecclesiastes 7:9). By being quick to anger shows that one may be over-reacting to the situation. The wise person would avoid any hasty reactions. Here Solomon uses the word "spirit" which is the inner state of mind. Therefore, as a Christian I am to keep my temper under control.

Solomon stated, "Make no friendship with an angry man; and with a furious man thou shall not go" (Proverbs 22:24). Those who are suffering from Post Traumatic Stress Disorder have few friends. Would you want to be a friend to a person who is angry? Paul states, "Be ye angry, and sin not: let not the sun go down upon your wrath" (Ephesians 4:6). This passage gave me a lot of trouble. This passage is saying that I can be angry and not sin but if I do sin I am not to "let the sun go down upon your [my] wrath." If I become angry I must correct the damage that I had done quickly. Before becoming a Christian I tried to justify my anger. "I have the right to be angry" was the lie that I told myself. Why do I have the right to be? "Because the Army took two years of my life away from me" was the answer. But that was my duty and it was an honor to serve my country. I volunteered to be drafted. "Because the Army sent me to Vietnam for one year" was the answer. But, I volunteered to go to Vietnam. In reality, I lost two years of my life that cannot be replaced. Thinking about that makes my anger indicator go up. But then I think of the years that I lost while not serving the Lord. Sobering!

What good came out of those two years? I met the bravest men that I would ever get to know. They suffered and sacrificed and were stripped of their humanity just like me. We did not pick one another. The trust that we have given to one another is known by no other person. I carry their memory in my mind and they carry the memory of me in theirs. I have "brothers" all over the United States.

What good came out of those two years? I got an education. I used my GI Bill to study the Bible. The association and fellowship with all the Christians that I came in contact with was overwhelming. I have had "fathers" and "mothers" and "brothers" and "sisters" scattered all over the world. I am a part of "God's Family."

But what was I to do with this anger? I studied 1 Corinthians 10:11-12 over and over. "Now all these things happened unto them for ensamples: and they are written for our admonition, upon whom the ends of the world are come. Wherefore let him that thinketh he standeth take heed lest he fall." I never wanted to be that person of 1967 and 1968 again! I kept telling myself that if hell is anything like Vietnam, I do not want to go there for an eternity. In reality I could fall. Why did these fall? "Let us labour therefore to enter into that rest, <u>lest any man fall after the same example of unbelief</u>" (Hebrews 4:11). I looked hard at the word "unbelief." I knew that I wanted to remain a believer! But how could I preach, teach, and live as a Christian with all of this anger still in my mind (heart)?

"For it became him, for whom are all things, and by whom are all things, in bringing many sons unto glory, to make the captain of their salvation perfect through sufferings" (Hebrews 2:10). The word "perfect" is from the Greek word $\tau\epsilon\lambda\epsilon\iota o\omega$ and means, "to make perfect, complete...add what is yet wanting in order to render a thing full...to bring to the end (goal) proposed...." (Strong G5048). We are all what we are because of what we have gone through in life. Out of all that we have been through, our life is what we make it. Sergeant Bixen was a wise man. He had said, "You only have one life, make the best of it. You only have one life to live." I could not make the best of my life because of anger that I had in my mind (heart). I had to get rid of this anger.

Paul wrote, "Let all bitterness, and wrath, and anger, and clamour, and evil speaking, be put away from you, with all malice" (Ephesians 4:31). Let it be "put away from you." That's me! The Greek word here is $\alpha\pi\theta\eta\tau\omega$ (Strong G142) and means, "to raise up, elevate, lift up…to bear away what has been raised." Paul is saying let it be lifted up from you. It is to be removed. How? Paul said,

> "Lie not one to another, <u>seeing that ye have put off the old man with his deeds</u>; And have put on the new man, which is renewed in knowledge after the image of him that created him: Where there is neither Greek nor Jew, circumcision nor uncircumcision, Barbarian, Scythian, bond nor free: but Christ is all, and in all. Put on therefore, as the elect of God, holy and beloved, bowels of mercies, kindness, humbleness of mind, meekness, longsuffering; Forbearing one another, and forgiving one another, if any man have a quarrel against any: even as Christ forgave you, so also do ye. And above all these things put on charity, which is the bond of perfectness. And let the peace of God rule in your hearts, to the which also ye are called in one body; and be ye thankful. <u>Let the word of Christ dwell in you</u> richly in all wisdom; teaching and admonishing one another in psalms and hymns and spiritual songs, singing with grace in your hearts to the Lord" (Colossians 3:9–16).

It was simple. If you put something off, replace it by putting something on.

My anger had to be controlled because of what the word of God taught. I listened to God as He spoke to Cain.

> "And the LORD said unto Cain, Why art thou wroth? and why is thy countenance fallen? If thou doest well, shalt thou not be accepted? and if thou doest not well, sin lieth at the door. And unto thee

shall be his desire, and thou shalt rule over him" (Genesis 4:6-7).

Solomon wrote, "He that hath no rule over his own spirit Is like a city that is broken down, and without walls" (Proverbs 25:28). In addition, he also stated, "A fool uttereth all his mind: But a wise man keepeth it in till afterwards" (Proverbs 29:11). But how could I control my anger? I listened to the wise man! "A soft answer turneth away wrath: but grievous words stir up anger" (Proverbs 15:1). "The beginning of strife is as when one letteth out water: therefore leave off contention, before it be meddled with" (Proverbs 17:14). "He that hath knowledge spareth his words: and a man of understanding is of an excellent spirit. Even a fool, when he holdeth his peace, is counted wise: and he that shutteth his lips is esteemed a man of understanding" (Proverbs 17:27–28).

Do I ever get angry? Yes. Paul said, "Be ye angry, and sin not: let not the sun go down upon your wrath" (Ephesians 4:26). My thorn in the flesh is Post Traumatic Stress Disorder (PTSD) and my replacement therapy is, "Pleasing The Savior Daily."

Chapter 9

Anxiety Reactions

"Don't worry, be happy!" Every time I remember this I grin.

As one who suffers from Post Traumatic Stress Disorder my autonomic senses are tuned to anything out of the ordinary. Before Linda and I were married we were looking at a display of furniture in one of the furniture stores when all of a sudden the street sweeper backfired. I hit the ground! I found that it was also hard for me to go into a crowd. I felt uncomfortable having people walking real close behind me. Even standing out in the opening brought anxiety. It was hard to sit in front of people. It seemed that I always wanted to be next to the wall facing the door. I reverted back to my early school day when I was told to "sit in the corner." After Vietnam, I didn't mind "sitting in the corner." Why the corner? I could observe everybody and everything.

All of these were my survival techniques. Survival? "Hey wake up you are not in Vietnam." As a combat veteran I felt threatened. These techniques are hard to give up. Many of us had/have weapons to protect ourselves. Since my family liked to campout, Linda wanted to campout with them. I had been home from Vietnam about ten months. One night in our tent Linda was fixing my bed and she told me that there was a rock under my pillow. I quickly replied, "That's not a rock, it's my pistol."

While at Memphis School of Preaching we had a discussion in class one day about weapons. I kept quiet and kept my opinion to myself. But one of my classmates asked me what I thought. I stated that I had a pistol in my apartment. He asked me why. I tried to explain but I do not think he got the point because he asked me, "What would you do if someone broke into your apartment?" I replied, "Come over tonight and knock down the front door and see." I no longer own a firearm!

Loud noises, certain sounds, and smells are those things that threaten and cause anxiety reactions. Why do we react the way that we do? It is because of feelings of uncertainty of what is about to happen or is happening. "Where is the bunker?" I need a place to hide! It may also be feelings of helplessness. "Where is my weapon?" "Do I have enough ammo?" "Where is the air support?" I need to protect myself! "Do you hear that?" The sound of the helicopter coming to pick you up to carry you out into the jungle or bring you back to the base camp brings mixed reactions. "Do you smell that?" We used diesel fuel to burn the human waste.

It is said of God's coming in Psalms 77:17-18, "The clouds poured out water: The skies sent out a sound: Thine arrows also went abroad. The voice of thy thunder *was* in the heaven: The lightning's lightened the world: The earth trembled and shook." I never remember it thundering or lightning in Vietnam but during the monsoon season the "clouds poured out water." During the Battle of Sui Cut on January 1st, 1968 the "thundering" of the bombing and shelling of our perimeter "trembled and shook" our foxholes. The "tracers" from all that was flying above "lightened the world" like "lightning." Even to this day, I have anxiety reactions when I hear loud thunder and see a streak of lightning, my mind goes back to Sui Cut! When the rain pours it brings anxiety reactions of our fighting during the monsoon season.

Jeremiah wrote in 6:17, "Also I set watchmen over you, *saying*, Hearken to the sound of the trumpet. But they said, We will not hearken." The trumpet has its own sound, so do the "tubes" that the VC (Viet Cong) uses to fire their mortars. That "thump" sound never leaves you. On August 17th, 1968, I and five other "short timers" volunteered to go out to Fire Support Base Buell II so that the artillerymen could get some rest. We all got rest until about 10 PM. The VC (Viet Cong) and NVA (North Vietnamese Army) began the battle of Tay Ninh. I had only thirteen days left in Vietnam. What made me volunteer? They were my "brothers." I knew what it was like not to sleep for long periods of time. I had already pulled my two hours of guard duty. I was behind the foxhole about twenty-five feet half way asleep when I heard "thump", "thump", "thump": there was that "tube" sound of the

VC (Viet Cong). Five of us ran for the foxhole yelling "incoming." We stayed in the foxhole all night and the artillery fired directly into the on-coming enemy. Our responses to the sounds and smells of Vietnam were learned reactions (behaviors).

I had to analyze my reactions to these sounds and smells. I would also have to focus on the consequences of how I respond to any sudden "threats." When I hear certain sounds I tell myself over and over "you are not in Vietnam." Knowing that I was not in Vietnam meant that what I was hearing or smelling was not a real threat.

Do I still jump or hit the ground when I hear loud noises? Yes. Do I still think of burning human waste when I smell diesel fuel? Yes. But I know where I am. I am home in the United States of America and I am preparing for my eternal home in heaven. My thorn in the flesh is Post Traumatic Stress Disorder (PTSD) and my focus is on "Pleasing The Savior Daily."

Chapter 10

Sleep Disturbance/Nightmares

"When were you in Vietnam?" One would expect the date you entered and the date you left Vietnam. But often two words are stated. "Last night." The average night sleep for the combat soldier in the field was three to four hours a night.

In Vietnam when we were out on an operation before dark we would setup a perimeter by digging a foxhole. Usually three men occupied the foxhole. Also a LP (Listening Post) of three men would be sent out in front of each platoon. The sleep arrangements were often left up to the men occupying the foxhole or on the LP (Listening Post). We usually took one hour watches. This would mean that we would get at least one or two hours before our watch. This habit became a way of life in the veteran even after he got home and got out of the military.

While on guard you did not want to be caught asleep by anyone, especially "Charlie"! One would fight sleep until they just could not stay awake. Then you would wake the next person and tell them that you cannot stay awake. This behavior was/is hard to unlearn.

Veterans struggle with sleep disturbance and nightmares. Many of us stay awake as long as it is possible. We have to occupy our minds or they begin to wander back to our tour of duty. We will watch television until we fall asleep in our chair, sofa, or on the floor. We will even watch re-runs over and over!

Even when we fall asleep, we begin to dream or have nightmares. What do we dream? Sometimes we dream of the actual events that happened and at other times it is a mixture of the past and the present. Many of our dreams are the same night after night. In the dream we are actually in Vietnam. The veteran usually tosses and turns all during the night. Night sweats are very prominent. Some will scream and yell in their sleep.

One of my greatest fears in Vietnam was being captured. In "The Group" we were relating events that happened in Vietnam and one of the men told of his being chased back into the perimeter by the VC (Viet Cong). He went out to get his claymore mine and when he looked up he saw them coming. He escaped by running "faster than I had ever run in my life." A few weeks later, I had a nightmare. I was in Vietnam and I was being chased by the VC (Viet Cong). They were about the catch me when Linda grabbed my arm and began screaming to awaken me. Well in my nightmare the VC (Viet Cong) caught me! Linda said that I was running in the bed and making all kinds of noises. This never happened to me in Vietnam. Then why did I dream it? Fear of being captured is the only answer. Linda learned a valuable lesson: do not touch Bobby when he is dreaming. Now, she screams out, "Bobby, wake up you are dreaming!"

Solomon said, "When thou liest down, thou shalt not be afraid: Yea, thou shalt lie down, and thy sleep shall be sweet" (Proverbs 3:24). Here the word "afraid" refers to any kind of fright, threat, dread, or terror (Strong H6342). The word "sweet" is used in the sense of sound, peaceful, and pleasant sleep (Strong H6149). Oh, how I yearn for this kind of sleep, where at night I could lie down and peacefully sleep without dreaming or having a nightmare. Even after a "good night's sleep" I am still very tired.

"The fear of the wicked, it shall come upon him: But the desire of the righteous shall be granted" (Proverbs 10:24). The word fear means "fear, terror" (Strong H4034). As one who suffers from Post Traumatic Stress Disorder this means a fear that is so intense that it results in screaming out at night and even getting up to get away from whatever it is that one is dreaming. However, I am not wicked! Why am I having these dreams, nightmares? It is my "desire" to overcome the dreams and nightmares of my past. Solomon said that my desire "shall be granted" if I am "of the righteous." Pleasing The Savior Daily!

Eliphaz said,

"In thoughts from the visions of the night, When deep sleep falleth on men, Fear came upon me, and trembling, Which made all my bones to shake. Then a spirit passed before my face; The hair of my flesh stood up" (Job 4:13-15).

Eliphaz tells of the fear that came upon him to the point that his entire body was trembling. This describes the mental and physical reaction of a nightmare. We all have heard and probably said the same thing that Eliphaz said, "The hair of my flesh stood up." This is a natural reaction to a frightening experience.

Job responds to God, "When I say, My bed shall comfort me, My couch shall ease my complaint; Then thou scarest me with dreams, And terrifiest me through visions…" (Job 7:13-14). Many times I would think that if I could only go to bed and go to sleep my thoughts of Vietnam would go away. In my anguish I was hoping to find comfort and relief but this did not happen. It seemed like I could not escape. If I am awake my thoughts were back in Vietnam and if I went to bed, dreams and nightmares would follow. The dreams and nightmares were frightening.

The Psalmist said, "How are they brought into desolation, as in a moment! They are utterly consumed with terrors" (Psalm 73:19). The Hebrew for "terrors" means, "terror, destruction, calamity, dreadful event." (Strong H1091). The "terrors" in this verse probably refer the terrors of death. Death had become a way of life in Vietnam and now the dreams and nightmares bring back those who died. When I visited The Wall (The Vietnam Memorial Wall) in Washington, D. C. not only did I see and feel of the names but I saw their faces. Faces of those wounded and those who died do not escape my dreams.

Daniel said. "I saw a dream which made me afraid, and the thoughts upon my bed and the visions of my head troubled me" (Daniel 4:5). Awaking from my dreams and nightmares my heart would be racing and my body would be sweating. I would be screaming as loud as I could. Sometimes I just could not escape them. I was troubled because it had gotten to the point where it was getting harder to awaken myself. The dreams and nightmares brought depression, survivals guilt, and fear. All of the symptoms of Post Traumatic Stress Disorder produce each other.

Jesus said,

> "Come unto me, all *ye* that labour and are heavy laden, and I will give you rest. Take my yoke upon you, and learn of me; for I am meek and lowly in heart: and ye shall find rest unto your souls. For my yoke *is* easy, and my burden is light" (Matthew 11:28-30).

The word "rest" is from the Greek word $\alpha\nu\alpha\tau\alpha\upsilon\omega$ and it means, "1 to cause or permit one to cease from any movement or labour in order to recover and recollect his strength. 2 To give rest, refresh, to give one's self rest, take rest. 3 to keep quiet, of calm and patient expectation" (Strong G373). Paul wrote, "I can do all things through Christ which strengtheneth me" (Philippians 4:13).

Do I still have dreams and nightmares of Vietnam? Yes! Each night I read my Bible. Upon retiring to my bed many times I fall asleep while praying. What do I do when I am awakened by a dream or nightmare? I talk to myself and/or pray until I fall back to sleep. I remember what the Psalmist said, "He will not suffer thy foot to be moved: He that keepeth thee will not slumber. Behold, he that keepeth Israel shall neither slumber nor sleep" (Psalm 121:3-4). God is on guard and He will not slumber nor will He go to sleep. My thorn in the flesh is Post Traumatic Stress Disorder (PTSD) and rest is needed for me to be about "Pleasing The Savior Daily."

Chapter 11

Flashbacks

"You've never lived till you've almost died. For those who fight for it, life [some say "freedom"] has a flavor that the protected will never know." (Author Unknown).

What are flashbacks? They are memories of past traumatic events in one's life. This definition applies to all people. Flashbacks bring about panic, the feeling of being trapped, and feeling powerless. Why do flashbacks occur? It is my belief that they occur because I had to insulate myself from the emotional and physical horrors of Vietnam. Those horrors remained isolated and I was unable to express my true feelings and thoughts. When they occurred, I forgot about being a Christian because I was not a Christian when they happened. But in Pleasing The Savior Daily I know I have the reassurance that, "There hath no temptation taken you but such as is common to man: but God *is* faithful, who will not suffer you to be tempted above that ye are able; but will with the temptation also make a way to escape, that ye may be able to bear *it*" (1 Corinthians 10:13). The intense feelings of a flashback are so frightening because the feelings are not related to the reality of what's going on right now. Those who experience them feel out of control. Here's where I have learned to tell myself "this is not real" and find something that is real, like a wall, and lean on it. We begin to avoid anything that stimulates a flashback. Vietnam veterans have come to realize that flashbacks are "normal."

"Smelling diesel fuel sends me back to Nam." "I don't like surprising loud noises because they make me think of Vietnam." "I cannot watch "war" movies or movies with certain weapons being used because I find myself back over there." Many other expressions could be sited but these helps one to understand that a veteran who is suffering from Post Traumatic Stress Disorder may have a flashback just from smelling diesel fuel, being surprised by a loud noise or just watching a war movie from Hollywood. I have had a number of flashbacks since leaving Vietnam in 1968.

Linda and I went to a movie. Simple! No, not for the veteran because being in a crowded place is not "simple." The movie had not started but they were giving previews of upcoming movies. In one of the previews a man shot a RPG (rocket propelled grenade) at someone. As I was tensing up Linda said, "It's only a movie Bobby." Realizing what she said she then took my hand. Then I knew I was with my wife in a movie theatre and not in the Village of Apo Cho February 7th, 1968. It was just a movie, but if you ever had a RPG shot at you then you would understand. A RPG round was used to blow up a tank. I weighed only 160 pounds and here comes a RPG round at my chest. It explodes behind me. I felt blood running down my face where the shrapnel had hit me. I would have been blown into hundreds of pieces if Sergeant Jones had not jumped up and motioned for me to get down. He died and I lived.

As a Vietnam veteran who has been in counseling since 1997 I have learned some things that have helped me.

I had to recognize that what I was having was a flashback to Vietnam. Then I tell myself when (if I can remember when) it took place. I remind myself that any decision I made then was a 19 year old making it. I remind myself that I survived and that now is the time to let go of the terror, panic, hurt, survivals guilt, and rage. Getting a firm grip or making sure your feet are on solid ground because it is not a time to run, it's a time to take a stand. I breathe. I use my five senses to orient myself to the present. I see the room. I listen for the sounds. I touch my face, arms, and legs. I acknowledge where I am. I talk to the 19 year old Gayton. I have found self-talk to be the most helpful outside of prayer. Why self-talk? I remind myself what the Bible says,

> "Who shall separate us from the love of Christ? *shall* tribulation, or distress, or persecution, or famine, or nakedness, or peril, or sword? As it is written, For thy sake we are killed all the day long; we are accounted as sheep for the slaughter. Nay, in all these things we are more than conquerors through him that loved us. For I am persuaded, that neither

death, nor life, nor angels, nor principalities, nor powers, nor things present, nor things to come, Nor height, nor depth, nor any other creature, shall be able to separate us from the love of God, which is in Christ Jesus our Lord" (Romans 8:35-39).

In 1992, we started the Vietnam Veterans of Bartow County (Cartersville, Georgia). Only those veterans who went to Vietnam were able to join. We begin to see the need for counseling even though we all were helping one another deal with our Vietnam experience. As you know many of us had PhD's from South Vietnam University with clusters located all over South Vietnam. Many of those in our group "majored" in combat! We went to the Atlanta Vet Center and sought help. We have a Vet Center located in our county. The counselor is a Vietnam veteran and he comes once a week to counsel with all veterans and their spouses. This is our support system. We also know that help from one of our "brothers" is only a call away. "My brothers" numbers are on my cell phone. After every flashback that I have experience it has taken weeks to get back to where I was. I have come to appreciate myself for being able to overcome the beating that I use to give myself. It has taken me a long time to get where I am today. There has been one virtue that I know that I always need help with and that is patience. I want what I want right now especially about my Vietnam experience. I have figured it out according to my doctor: I am not crazy! My thorn in the flesh is Post Traumatic Stress Disorder (PTSD) and I am healing by "Pleasing The Savior Daily!"

Chapter 12

Intrusive Thoughts

Would Eve be able to forget the violence that was cause by her son Cain?

> "And Adam knew his wife again; and she bare a son, and called his name Seth: For God, *said she*, hath appointed me another seed instead of Abel, whom Cain slew. And to Seth, to him also there was born a son; and he called his name Enos: then began men to call upon the name of the LORD" (Genesis 4:25-26).

Here is a happy time in the life of Eve but she could not forget Cain's violence and Abel's death. But, Eve could recover. God knows where we are. "Neither is there any creature that is not manifest in his sight: but all things *are* naked and opened unto the eyes of him with whom we have to do" (Hebrews 4:13).

The combat veteran's life is troubled. Jesus told Martha "thou art careful and troubled about many things..." (Luke 10:41-42). Peter wrote, "Casting all your care upon Him; for He careth for you" (1 Peter 5:7). David said, "The LORD also will be a refuge for the oppressed, A refuge in the times of trouble" (Psalm 9:9). The Psalmist said, "Give us help from trouble: For vain is the help of man" (Psalm 60:11). David wrote, "And hide not they face from thy servant; For I am in trouble: hear me speedily" (Psalm 69:17). Asaph in speaking of God wrote, "Thou calledst in trouble, and I delivered thee; I answered thee in the secret place of thunder..." (Psalm 81:7). There are times that the combat veteran could say with David, "Trouble and anguish have taken hold on me..." (Psalm 119:143). The combat veteran prays like David did in Psalm 143:11. "Quicken me, O LORD, for thy name's sake: For thy righteousness' sake bring my soul out of trouble." Solomon said, "The righteous is delivered out of trouble...But the just shall come out of trouble" (Proverbs 11:8; 12:13). Jesus told His disciples, "Let not your heart be troubled..." (John 14:1).

Some of the common stress reactions relevant to the combat veteran include the things that I have already discussed but there are others such as excessive drinking, drug use, uncontrolled and frequent crying, physical illnesses, difficulties with concentrating and suicidal thoughts and plans. Yes, the combat veteran's life is troubled.

The traumatic memories that we have of the battles and firefights have been replayed over and over in our minds. What are we doing? We are searching for an alternative outcome of what actually happened in Vietnam. We are very hard on ourselves because we wonder what we could have done to change some of it so that it would turn out different. When reality sets in, then follows the guilt feeling and then comes depression. It seems like an endless battle.

Why is it that the common things that happen every day where we live reminds us of Vietnam or any other traumatic event in our life?

I have heard helicopters come over my house and my thoughts are "they are coming to get us and take us out of this place." Then I start singing the song of the Animals, "We've got to get out of this place if it's the last thing we ever do." Many of the songs of the sixties' remind us of Vietnam! Is that the reason we listen to them?

Why is it that the smell of urine will bring back thoughts of Vietnam? Because the corpses have no muscle tone and the bladder evacuates at the moment of death. Why it is that the smell of diesel fuel brings back our memories of our base camp? Because the commodes and latrines contained diesel fuel and were burned when filled.

While at the Memphis School of Preaching, I preached at the Hughes, Arkansas congregation. As Linda, Brooke, and I would travel from Memphis to Hughes we saw a lot of tree lines and rice fields. I remember telling them that it reminded me of Vietnam. On our twenty-fifth wedding anniversary we traveled from Cartersville,

Georgia to the Ozarks. Over and over my thoughts went to Vietnam and the times that we were fired upon from the tree lines as we were crossing the rice paddies.

Many of us have tried to avoid things that bring back intrusive thoughts. I have been a "troubled" Vietnam combat veteran. I also have been a "troubled" Christian wanting to work out all the symptoms of Post Traumatic Stress Disorder in my life. I have found that it is easier to face them as I can. To remind myself that those things are in the past and that I cannot allow them to destroy the now nor the future. I did not want to remain "numb" and avoid these things anymore. But there are the constant reminders of my time in Vietnam. It's something that I will never forget.

When I first went to a VA psychiatrist I was asked, "Are you suicidal?" My answer was the answer of a friend who had open heart surgery and while recovering he had a stroke that paralyzed his left side. If that was not enough, his wife left him and their two children. When asked by the psychiatrist, "Are you suicidal?" He said, "I loves' me too much to do that." That was the response that I gave to the VA psychiatrist. I also told her that suicide was contrary to what I believed and that, "If hell is anything like Vietnam, I did not want to go there." Every time a veteran goes to the VA or to the VA Clinic they are asked, "Are you suicidal?" Suicide is a permanent solution for a temporary problem. Post Traumatic Stress Disorder is a temporary problem that one can live with if they obtain help. My thorn in the flesh is Post Traumatic Stress Disorder (PTSD) and I have found my help in "Pleasing The Savior Daily."

CHAPTER 13

The Conscience

Paul wrote to Timothy the following words,

This charge I commit unto thee, son Timothy, according to the prophecies which went before on thee, that thou by them mightest war a good warfare; Holding faith, and a good conscience; which some having put away concerning faith have made shipwreck:" (1 Timothy 1:18–19).

Webster defines conscience as "a: the sense or consciousness of the moral goodness or blameworthiness of one's own conduct, intentions, or character together with a feeling of obligation to do right or be good; b: a faculty, power, or principle enjoining good acts; c: the part of the superego in psychoanalysis that transmits commands and admonitions to the ego…" The Greek word συνειδεσις, is defined as, "1 the consciousness of anything. 2 the soul as distinguishing between what is morally good and bad, prompting to do the former and shun the latter, commending one, condemning the other. 2A the conscience" (Strong G489).

Each of us has an urge to act in harmony with what we believe to be morally right. Our conscience acts to prod us to do what we believe to be right and to avoid that which is wrong. Our conscience is dependent upon our standard of morality.

I have already mentioned Paul (Saul), but he is an excellent example of how the conscience works. Luke writes,

"Then they cried out with a loud voice, and stopped their ears, and ran upon him with one accord, And cast *him* out of the city, and stoned *him*: and the witnesses laid down their clothes at a young man's feet, whose name was Saul. And they stoned Stephen, calling upon *God*, and saying, Lord Jesus, receive my spirit. And he kneeled down, and cried with a loud voice, Lord, lay not this sin to their charge. And when he had said this, he fell asleep. And Saul was consenting unto his death. And at that time there was a great persecution against the church which was at Jerusalem; and they were all scattered abroad throughout the regions of Judaea and Samaria, except the apostles" (Acts 7:57-8:1).

Paul's (Saul's) conscience was not violated as he was "consenting" to the death of Stephen. The word "consenting" comes from the Greek word is συνευδοκεω and is defined as, "1 to be pleased together with, to approve together (with others). 2 to be pleased at the same time with, consent, agree to. 2A to applaud" (Strong G4909). It is hard for us to see him as this type of man. Luke in Acts 8:3 says, "As for Saul, he made havock of the church, entering into every house, and haling men and women committed *them* to prison." He made "havock" of the church that means "...to affix a stigma to, to dishonour, spot, defile...to treat shamefully or with injury, to ravage, devastate, ruin" (Strong G3075). Can you picture the man who by the Holy Spirit wrote the majority of the New Testament doing this to the Lord's church? Paul says of himself that he was "a blasphemer, and a persecutor, and injurious" man (1 Timothy 1:13). He also admits in this passage that he "did it ignorantly in unbelief." What about his conscience? Paul said, "Men *and* brethren, I have lived in all good conscience before God until this day" (Acts 23:1). How could this be? Paul acts in harmony with what he believed to be morally right. His conscience prodded him to do what he believed to be right. Later in Paul's life he looks back in shame at what he had done to the Lord's work. "This *is* a faithful saying, and worthy of all acceptation, that Christ Jesus came into the world to save sinners; of whom I am chief" (1 Timothy 1:15). What happened? Paul's moral standard changed.

I can only speak for myself as a combat Vietnam veteran; I violated my conscience, my moral standard. As I saw my "brothers" being wounded, maimed, and killed, my conscience hardened to the very fact that I did not respect the lives of my enemy. I thought when I became a Christian that my war was over but it had just begun. The Bible speaks of the war between the flesh (the outward man) and the spirit (the inner man). (Romans 7:18-8:13). My thorn in the flesh, Post Traumatic Stress Disorder (PTSD), was my war! I wanted to justify what I had done in Vietnam, but the more I studied the Bible I knew that the only justification was "it was a war" and that does not take away the memories of it. As a Christian I have a "new life" because I am a "new person" with a "new loyalty."

The Bible teaches me that I am to have a "good conscience" (1 Timothy 1:5, 19). Timothy was told, "Holding the mystery of the faith in a pure conscience" (1 Timothy 3:9; cf. 2 Timothy 1:3). How may I maintain my conscience? By giving consideration to all of my actions, I will give my conscience an opportunity to work. Paul said, "Prove all things; hold fast that which is good. Abstain from all appearance of evil" (1 Thessalonians 5:21-22). The conscience is a powerful tool. Knowledge is power. My thorn in the flesh is Post Traumatic Stress Disorder (PTSD) and I if I teach my conscience the knowledge of God's word; I know I am "Pleasing The Savior Daily."

CHAPTER 14

This and That

Vietnam in Perspective

By George "Sonny" Hoffman

Intelligent, rational human beings have difficulty accepting the U.S. involvement in Southeast Asia. I had trouble. Aside from the involvement issue, our conduct of the war seemed even more indefensible. No-fire zones, free-fire zones, bombing restrictions, and the ubiquitous rules of engagement defied reason. To look at the Vietnam War in isolation also defies reason.

The war was never fought to win. That is an absurdity to most people, veterans especially. The strategy was to contain the spread of global communism. This may seem laughable in light of the fall of communism, but no one was laughing in the fifties and sixties as country after country fell behind the iron and bamboo curtains. Communism was perceived as a serious threat to our national security. The threat of a global nuclear war loomed on the horizon, and we had come close several times before the first troops landed in Vietnam. The demise of humanity, indeed, all life on Earth, teetered on the brink of annihilation. Statesmen on both sides had this reality to deal with.

It was in this atmosphere of fear and insecurity that our leaders decided to draw a line in the jungle. Clearly, a line needed to be drawn somewhere. Once that line was drawn, it needed to be defended. The world watched to check our resolve. We held that line for 10,000 days. As a delaying action, it was quite successful. By tying the communists down in Southeast Asia, we bought valuable time. Other countries successfully resisted insurgency movements as the weakness inherent in the rigid socialist systems began to show. When we no longer needed to defend the line in the jungle, we pulled out. By then, communism was no longer on the march. If anything, it was on the defensive.

As to our irrational and irresponsible conduct of the war, I submit that is was neither. Counter-insurgency warfare is a tricky business. It is more political than military. In the post Napoleonic era, theory returned to war as a rational, limited instrument of national diplomacy. This approach was best articulated by the Prussian military theorist, Carl von Clausewitz. He set the tone of modern armed conflict in his 1837 book, On War. It was he who stated, "War is the natural extension of diplomacy," and that "War, followed to its natural conclusion, is total."

In the aftermath of two global wars and the advent of nuclear weapons, his words took on greater significance. Military planners and statesmen on both sides read the book and bought into the philosophy. The cold war was fought using his book as a guide. The Vietnam rules of engagement were a direct result of this philosophy. Who can say whether he was right or wrong? The fact remains that we did not annihilate mankind in a nuclear holocaust, and China did not invade as they did in Korea. Our strategists had to carefully maneuver the tactics to straddle these two main concerns.

To be viewed correctly, Vietnam must be seen in the context of a much bigger war--the Cold War. Vietnam was one battle in a very long war. Even if you accept the popular notion that the U.S. lost that battle--which I do not--we, never-the-less, won the war. The Union soldiers that fought at Fredericksburg during our Civil War undeniably lost that battle. Some of those men were in the parade down Pennsylvania Avenue at the war's end. They had the satisfaction of knowing that their comrades did not die in vain. They were winners, not losers, even if Fredericksburg was the only battle they fought.

Vietnam, as big as it seemed to those of us involved in the fighting, was a minor skirmish. The losses were insignificant to what was at stake. Fifty-eight thousand placed on one scale against five billion on the other, makes it insignificant. I cringe at the notion that those lives were wasted, sacrificed in vain. If anything, no warrior ever gave a life for so noble a cause or sacrificed it for so many. Indeed, Churchill's words about the RAF ring true for the veterans of Vietnam: "Never have so many owed so much too so few."

I have no doubt that when the world looks back on the twentieth century with crystal vision, Vietnam will be seen for what it was: the turning point of the greatest threat humanity ever faced-- communism. If you had a part in the Vietnam War, take pride, hold your head high. When you visit The Wall, revere those names etched thereon. If you cannot see their glory, your great grandchildren will.

"For Those who fought for it,
Freedom has a Flavor,
The Protected will never know"

(George "Sonny" Hoffman. He served three tours in Vietnam).

My Song
One Year Tour
Let me tell a story, I can tell it well
How we spent a year in a place like hell
We went to a country far from home
It was called South Vietnam
[Chorus] We longed for home never more to roam
And "If You're Going To San Francisco" was a favorite song
Well we went to the jungle nearly every day
But I longed for the pine trees and Georgia's red clay
We swam the rice patties to Saigon
But I rather been on Altoona just having some fun
[Chorus] I longed for home never more to roam
And "Georgia On My Mind" was my favorite song
We fought up and down Highway One
Oh how I wished for US 41
We were just grunts trying to stay alive
For I wanted to be living on Etowah Drive
[Chorus] I longed for home never more to roam
And "Georgia On My Mind" was my favorite song
We fought in TET of 1968
Many times we were at death's gate

We went to a city; Apo Cho was its name
When I left there I wasn't the same
[Chorus] I longed for home never more to roam
And "Georgia On My Mind" was my favorite song
We saw the Black Virgin Mountain on the skyline
Oh Just to see Ladds near that home of mine
I can't describe all that I saw
But I have a memory of the Etowah
[Chorus] I longed for home never more to roam
And "Georgia On My Mind" was my favorite song
Well I went to The Wall and I cried
For there were the names and faces of "Brothers" of mine
Some are still missing we know for a fact
You'll never be forgotten and we want you back
[Chorus] They long for home never more to roam
And "America The Beautiful" would be their favorite song.

Bobby D. Gayton

MESSAGE FROM THE WALL

Grace and God has brought me here to visit with you Wall.
I'm trying hard to fight the tears. But they begin to fall.
I place my hands against the stone as if reaching for someone.
My head is bowed, my eyes are closed, my heart sounds like a drum.
"Why, why?" I asked. "Can anyone tell me why?"
The pain in my heart becomes a rage, as I continue to cry.
So many names, so young and brave, the world can never replace.
Surely there must be an answer for such a terrible waste.
Time has passed and I am weak. I can cry no more.
I've beat my fist against the ground, my knuckles are bleeding and sore.
Still with the question unanswered I feel that I must go.
But a voice began to speak to me from where I do not know.
"Stand Tall, Stand Tall," the voice said as if coming from the Wall.
Then it speaks again to me saying, "Veteran, Always Stand Tall."
I did not get an answer to the question, why?
But I'll carry the words within my heart until the day I die.
"Stand Tall, Stand Tall," my brother, is the message from the Wall.
Never let Vietnam happen again. Remember and always, "Stand Tall."

Lynda Moore, wife of N. C. Moore USMC Vietnam.

THE PURPLE HEART
(By the Daughter, the Sister and the Wife of Three Veterans)

The final chapter in a combat veteran's search for closure could be titled "The Purple Heart."

Post Traumatic Stress Disorder is a terrible condition. It causes mental anguish and physical illnesses. Permanent chemical changes occur in the brain of combat veterans caused by the sustained adrenalin their bodies produce during the lengthy time spent in combat situations.

For a veteran, this means a lifetime of mental struggle to overcome their symptoms. For some, the memories are the worst. The symptoms are often denial, self-pity, apathy, self-destruction, depression, anger or rage, and flashbacks. There can be symptoms such as insomnia, nightmares, night sweats, and emotional problems such as paranoia, mental collapse, and suicide.

Veterans often cannot relate to or develop a close relationship with their families. This hurts the veteran as much as their loved ones. Treatment includes drugs and therapy to learn coping techniques, but there is no "cure."

Physical illnesses such as diabetes, cancer, heart disease and a whole list of others have been identified as resulting from exposure to chemicals and sustained stress caused by PTSD.

The Purple Heart is presented to those who have shed their blood during combat. The physical scars will heal. The injury may cause disability and make life difficult. However, the true wound is to the spirit. This will never heal completely. Closure is just a word used to indicate the last chapter of a story. In real life, the story goes on. It lies in the minds and hearts of veterans everywhere. There is no "closure."

If you know or love a veteran, let him or her know that they deserve a "purple heart" for their spiritual wound just as much as for any physical one.

WELCOME HOME

Linda S. Gayton
February, 2001

CONCLUSION

All I ever wanted was to have inner peace. I discovered that what I wanted was a struggle to find and when I found it, it was a struggle to keep it. Jesus told the apostles, "Peace I leave with you, my peace I give unto you: not as the world giveth, give I unto you. Let not your heart be troubled, neither let it be afraid" (John 14:27). All the symptoms of Post Traumatic Stress Disorder prevented the inner peace that I so desired in life. To those who suffer from Post Traumatic Stress Disorder I say, "I know where you are going because I know where you have been."

Isaiah wrote, "Thou wilt keep *him* in perfect peace, *Whose* mind *is* stayed *on thee*: Because he trusteth in thee" (Isaiah 26:3). Paul wrote, "Therefore being justified by faith, we have peace with God through our Lord Jesus Christ" (Romans 5:1). My thorn in the flesh is Post Traumatic Stress Disorder (PTSD) and I get my inner peace from knowing that I am "Pleasing The Savior Daily."

WORKS CITED

All Bible quotations are taken from the *King James Version*.

American Psychiatric Association, *Diagnostic and Statistical Manual of Mental Disorders*, Fourth Edition. American Psychiatric Association, Washington 1994: 424-429.

Freeman, Arthur, *Cognitive Therapy*, p. 19 1987, Human Sciences Press, New York, NY.

Gayton, Linda Smith, *The Purple Heart*. Used By Permission.

Hoffman, George "Sonny", *Vietnam in Perspective*. Used By Permission.

Mish, Frederick C., *Merriam-Webster's Collegiate Dictionary* (Eleventh Edition).

Moore, Lynda, *The Stand Tall Poet*, "Message From The Wall," p. 15 1993. Vietnam Veterans of Bartow County. Used By Permission.

Strong, James, *The Exhaustive Concordance of the Bible:* Electronic ed. (Ontario: Woodside Bible Fellowship., 1996).

WELCOME HOME VIETNAM VETERANS!

**Over 2.6 Million Served
Over 58,000 Gave Their Lives
They Fought For Their Country
They Fought For Freedom
They Fought With Honor
In The End They Fought For Each Other
Harsh Words From Home
And Difficult Memories Have Faded
But Their Legacy Has Not.
WE WILL REMEMBER!
(Author Unknown)**

Bobby D. Gayton, 1967

**IF YOU ARE A VETERAN, THANK YOU
FOR SERVING OUR COUNTRY!
IF YOU ARE NOT A VETERAN, THANK YOU
FOR SUPPORTING OUR MILITARY!**

Made in the USA
Lexington, KY
29 September 2012